Lives and Legacies

of People With

Intellectual Disability

Kenneth D. Keith and Heather E. Keith

Published by
American Association on Intellectual and Developmental Disabilities
8403 Colesville Road, Suite 900
Silver Spring, MD 20910
www.aaidd.org

To order:
AAIDD Order Fulfillment
Phone: 202-387-1968 x 216
Email: books@aaidd.org
Online: http://aaidd.org/publications/bookstore-home

Product No. 4171
ISBN 978-0-9983983-2-7

Acknowledgments

This book became possible only with the help, patience, and support of many people. At the risk of overlooking someone, we want to express our gratitude for the contributions of Randy Bell, Joe Ebacher, Lisa Fennell, René Ferdinand, Steven Fesmire, Leslie Bishop Hartung, Connie Keith, Janet Miller, Tom Miller, David Powell, Lyn Rucker, and Bob Schalock. Special thanks are due our editor, Kathleen McLane, who encouraged and supported the project from beginning to end.

In memory of Eric, Mark, Mayo, Ollie, Ray, and Tom.
Their lives served to make us all better people.

"I am the same as you. I got a name, and I want you all to call me by my name."

—Ollie Webb (1928–2003)
Self-Advocate and Community Leader,
Omaha, Nebraska

Biographical Note: Ollie Webb was born during the Great Depression. At the age of 19, she was committed by her family to the Beatrice State Developmental Center in Nebraska. There she worked in the nursery, caring for infants and children, until she was discharged in the 1960s to live and work in a private nursing home in Omaha. In 1969, she met Tom Miller, whose job was to find people who had been discharged from the Center and make sure that their basic human rights were being respected. Through this connection, Ms. Webb secured a place to live in the community and took cooking classes, which led to a job with competitive pay that she held for 17 years and that gave her the opportunity to own her own home. She was a founding member of an Omaha self-advocacy organization and earned a national reputation for promoting self-advocacy. She overcame numerous emotional and physical adversities to live the life she wanted. In 2005, The ARC of Omaha and Career Solutions, Inc., merged and chose to name the new organization the Ollie Webb Center, Inc. to honor her and her life well-lived.

Table of Contents

Foreword

A Life of Quality and a Legacy of Value

Kenneth D. Keith and Heather E. Keith are well known for their significant contributions to the fields of intellectual disability (ID) and cross-cultural psychology. Their latest contribution on the lives and legacies of people with ID addresses an issue that is important to everyone: one's life and one's legacy.

Material presented in this book's well written and insightful nine chapters reflects five interrelated factors that have changed societal views and practices internationally regarding people with ID. These factors involve a commitment to the human and legal rights of people with disabilities as reflected in:

- the *United Nations Convention on the Rights of Persons with Disabilities: UNCRPD*
- a social-ecological model of disability that focuses on the interaction between individuals and the multiple factors at the micro, meso, and macro-system levels that affect human functioning and personal outcomes
- the use of personal support strategies that reduce the mismatch between a person's capabilities and the skills required by the environment for successful participation

- the quality-of-life concept with its emphasis on equity, inclusion, and empowerment, and its focus on the quality-of-life domains of personal development, self-determination, social inclusion, interpersonal relations, and emotional, physical, and material well-being; and
- the capability approach to disability that emphasizes the core values of freedom and human dignity and the conditions that a society creates to improve people's lives.

The approach described in this text is based on the values inherent in these interrelated factors. Chief among these values are the potential for all persons to grow, develop, and contribute to their society; the human and legal rights of people to live in least restrictive and safe environments, to participate fully in their communities, and to be contributing members of their society. A person's disability cannot be viewed in isolation, but rather is the result of an interaction between the person's capability and the environment's requirements and demands. With appropriate supports over time, human functioning can be enhanced; and the desire for a life of quality among all persons can be achieved.

As described and brought to life in this book through published material and individual stories, our understanding of ID has changed from a deficit or defect model to one emphasizing that each person has a unique blend of strengths and weaknesses. This understanding is based on society's commitment to improve people's lives through equal opportunities and individualized supports. Throughout the text, examples are provided of this evolution from dehumanization, abuse, and neglect to the achievement of a life of quality, self-advocacy, individualized supports, inclusive environments, and an emphasis on one's rights, choices, and community inclusion.

A truly unique contribution of this volume is to ask readers to consider the legacy of people with ID. To paraphrase Anton Chekhov, the authors stress that one's legacy should not pass by and retreat into eternity without a trace. So what is the trace that people with ID leave behind?

From all the people with ID and their families that I have known over the years, the trace/legacy they have left behind is the *integrity* they have shown in adapting to a less-than-desired situation and multiple challenges; the *knowledge* they have shared regarding their hopes, dreams, capability, potential, and coping strategies; and the *inspiration* that comes from seeing people overcome extreme challenges and continue to get up each morning to overcome the next challenge. From a societal and international perspective, the legacy of people with ID and their families has been the charge they have led for human and legal rights, equal opportunities, and the supports necessary to lead a life of quality; and the vision they have shared of ways to develop a new moral community rooted in respect for individuals and their rights to live in the community, to make personal decisions, and to be a part of a broader cultural understanding of people with a disability.

But perhaps their greatest legacy is value, which may seem counterfactual to how they have been treated in the past. After reading about the segregation of people with ID in institutions, the misuse of testing, the holocaust and extermination of people with a disability, and dying as "outsiders," readers of this volume will ask themselves what society can do to make sure that these types of treatments do not happen again. Addressing that question and developing a new moral community will be the legacy of this book.

To this end, the book is both proscriptive and prescriptive. Proscriptively, the authors examine the role of philosophy, psychology, medicine, and the broader community in creating cultural perspectives and legacies of people with ID that had often had their basis in stereotypes and misinformation. Prescriptively, the authors explore how the social construction of ID, the quality-of-life revolution, and the supports paradigm can work toward a new moral community rooted in respect for people with ID as equal. This ensures their personal rights, personal goals, and opportunities; and envisions a society in which people are recognized for what they can do rather than what they cannot. Fulfilling that prescription will enhance both the lives and legacies of people with ID.

Robert L. Schalock, Ph.D.

Preface

This book is an effort to construct a new way to view the cultural contributions, and their meaning, of the lives of people with intellectual disability (ID). This is not a book about end-of-life planning, coping with death and grief, or the process of dying and death, *per se*. Ultimately, each of us will be remembered for the roles we play with families, friends, and communities—for our contributions to those around us. We aim to show that the legacy of people with ID is as meaningful, as important, as any other—that their lives should not, in the words of writer Anton Chekhov, "pass by and retreat into eternity without a trace."

There is a wealth of resources available to psychologists, educators, caregivers, academics, and family members detailing how to care for and educate people with ID. There are also many publications on dehumanization and the quality of life of people with ID. We aim to add to those conversations with an exploration of the idea of the *legacy* of people with disability through their stories set within the social and cultural construction of the idea of disability, which is itself set within broader philosophic views about what makes us part of a moral community.

We believe that a book accessible to families of people with ID, as well as academics and practitioners, can be instrumental in moving toward a new moral community, one which enhances quality of life and better understands and celebrates the lives and legacies of people with ID. To this end we take an interdisciplinary approach that includes review of a wide range of relevant literature; a philosophical perspective on humanity, growth, and development; and stories of real people. We stress the importance of social context in defining ID, and the role of supports in ensuring participation of people with ID in the meaningful activity of everyday life. People with disability are a part of the fabric of every community, and their lives and contributions should likewise be a part of the legacy of their communities.

In the chapters that follow we discuss:

- what it means to be human and who should make decisions about the life, death, and humanity of people with ID
- the shameful ways that people with ID have died and sometimes been forgotten
- the social construction of ID and its implications for a new moral community
- the quality-of-life revolution and its contribution to a new moral community
- the supports movement and its role in the building of a new moral community
- the lives and legacies of real people
- the meaning in life and its contribution to living well and dying well

In the end, we believe that people with ID want, and can have, full lives embodying growth, relationships, and contributions to the community. They can live well, die well, and leave a legacy of dignity and respect.

KDK   HEK

Omaha, NE   Radford, VA

CHAPTER ONE

Introduction:
Thinking About Lives and Legacies

When Jon Will was born in 1972, a doctor asked his parents whether they intended to take him home—or would they send him to an institution? The question arose because Jon had Down syndrome, but it surprised Jon's parents, who naturally assumed that parents do indeed take their newborns home. Writing 40 years later, Jon's father, political columnist George Will, recounted the richness of Jon's life, including his love of major league baseball and his special connection with the Washington Nationals. The world, Will (2012) suggested, would be a better place if it were populated by more people with Down syndrome. Yet the attitude of the doctor, uncertain whether a child with Down syndrome would find a place in a family, has for too much of our history typified attitudes toward people with ID.

Death in the Midst of Life?

Traditional views of disability have had their basis in the notion that there exists a standard for normal functioning, and that deviations from that standard constitute disabilities (Barnes, 2016). Until the eighteenth century, the church applied the term "idiot" to anybody considered uneducated (Goodey, 2011)—people whom Pierre Charron (1707, p. 133) deemed "dead in the very midst of life." Philosophers have argued about the relative capacity of people with ID to engage in moral reasoning, and even about whether they are human. And in early America, the condition of ID was sometimes perceived as humorous, but at the same time considered deserving of compassion and Christian benevolence (Trent, 1994). But people with ID have not always been well-received by societies, and have often been the subject of efforts aimed toward the prevention or reversal of ID, segregation, or destruction (Wolfensberger, 1975). Perceptions of ID have long led to the labeling of people (e.g., Berkson, 2006; Evans, 1945; Keith & Keith, 2013), and their institutionalization (Wolfensberger, 1975).

Although many people with ID are well-treated by people without disabilities (e.g., Will, 2012), many others have long been subject to a variety of forms of victimization—criminal, financial, psychological, and sexual (Fisher, 2016). Older people may be at particular risk of abuse (e.g., Strasser, Smith, & O'Quin, 2016), and people with ID are far less likely than others to have regular interaction with friends or family members outside their homes (Bigby & Wiesel, 2011).

The Importance of Contact

In observations of brief encounters between people with ID and strangers in public spaces, Wiesel, Bigby, and Carling-Jenkins (2013) found that such encounters could be exclusionary or inclusionary, but were rarely truly convivial. This finding is unfortunate, in view of the fact that development of positive attitudes toward people with ID is associated with the experience of quality interactions between people with and without disability (Page & Islam, 2015). Similarly, although it can be difficult to recruit professionals in medical- and education-related disciplines to work with people with ID, one important factor related to their attitudes toward people with ID is prior acquaintance (Scior, 2011; Scior, Addai-Davis, Kenyon, & Sheridan, 2013; Werner & Grayzman, 2011)—knowing people with disability is important, and especially vital is the quality of interactions (Keith, Benetto, & Rogge, 2015). Still, medical students may be nervous about treating people with ID (Ryan & Scior, 2016), and practicing healthcare professionals may hold stigmatizing views (Pelleboer-Gunnink, Van Oorsouw, Van Weeghel, & Embregts, 2017).

Absent positive personal experience with people with ID, community members may stigmatize them, and as a result people with ID are too often subject to bullying and discrimination (e.g., Ali et al., 2015; McHugh & Howard, 2017). However, attitudes toward peers with ID may be more positive in school settings that are inclusive than in those that are not (Georgiadi, Kalyva, Kourkoutas, & Tsakiris, 2012), and among people who are younger and more highly educated (Morin, Rivard, Crocker, Boursier, & Caron, 2013). In addition, college students' perceptions of people with ID seem to become more negative as the age of the person with disability increases (Ahlbom, Panek, & Jungers, 2008). The latter finding is consistent with research reflecting negative attitudes toward aging in the general population (McConatha, Schnell, Volkwein, Riley, & Leach, 2003; Palmore, 1982), although the effect found by Ahlbom et al. was for people with ID at much younger ages.

What effects, we might wonder, do such findings suggest about aging people with ID, and, in keeping with the aim of this book, their legacies? The prospect of death, whether our own or that of loved ones, is not, for most people, a welcome idea; and anxiety and fear are common in the face of death (Gire, 2019). What do people with ID think about death, and how would they like to be remembered? These are questions we will explore in later chapters.

Lives and Legacies

As they pursue a good life, people with ID want essentially the same things from their lives that other people do (Morisse et al., 2013). Thus, it is reasonable to talk not only about life and its enhancement, but also about death and its meaning for individuals whose lives have not always been valued by their communities and their cultures.

What is a Legacy?

Perhaps we all would like to be remembered. What, when our lives are finished, do we hope to leave behind? The word *legacy*, with origins in medieval Latin, has enjoyed several meanings, including a sum of money left in a will, or a group of delegates representing someone important, like a king. However, the term can also mean a "tangible or intangible thing handed down by a predecessor; a long-lasting effect . . ." (*Shorter Oxford English Dictionary*, 2002, p. 1568). In addition to whatever worldly belongings we might leave to our heirs, we will also leave them with memories, perceptions, and a sense of who we are (were)—an intangible, long-lasting effect, a legacy. What any person's legacy will be is at least in part about the dignity of their ordinary or extraordinary life and their death.

Thinking About Death

Researchers have studied the understanding and perception of death of individuals with ID. McEvoy and his colleagues (McEvoy, 1989; McEvoy, MacHale, & Tierney, 2012), for example, found that most adults with ID had some understanding of death, including the fact that death is final and that all living things die. This understanding, however, was incomplete, and at least some individuals were thus vulnerable to factually incorrect beliefs. Despite sometimes limited understanding, research has shown that people with ID experience the grief associated with death (McEvoy, Treacy, & Quigley, 2017), responding to loss and bereavement similarly to people without ID (Mason & Dowling, 2016). Nevertheless, although community living staff agree that people with ID should know about death (Wiese, Dew, Stancliffe, Howarth, & Balandin, 2013), research by Wiese, Stancliffe, Dew, Balandin, and Howarth (2014) suggested that support staff may actually do little to assist those with ID to prepare for and deal with death, including how the dead may be remembered.

This is not to say that staff are not caring or moved by the death of their friends or clients with ID; for example, they may work with clergy or others conducting memorial services to assist them in use of appropriate disability terminology, thus protecting and honoring the memory of friends with ID, and they may help to establish such physical memorials as park benches or gardens to honor the deceased (e.g., Todd, 2013). Caregivers may also be so strongly emotionally attached to terminally ill people with ID that it is simply too overwhelming to talk about death (Tuffrey-Wijne et al., 2013). In fact, caregivers have expressed ambivalence and confusion concerning funeral arrangements for people with ID, and about whether (or how) to inform individuals with ID about the deaths of other people (Forrester-Jones, 2013). Moreover, the notion that people with ID might themselves leave a social legacy, that their deaths would create societal gaps and have powerful meaning for people who loved them, was slow to appear in the scholarly literature (Todd, Bernal, & Forrester-Jones, 2013).

What About the Past?

When the legacy of people with ID has been the subject of specific attention, it has often been as a case study in misunderstanding or abuse. Thus, when a man with Down syndrome died in police custody, a special training program for police became his "legacy" (Vargas, 2014), and the outcome of death penalty cases has sometimes been the legacy of people with ID who were charged with capital crimes (Sundby, 2014).

Some people with ID have succeeded in making lasting names for themselves in exemplary ways. For example, Raymond Loomis, as we will see in Chapter 8, became known as a strong, inspirational leader for self-advocates (Williams & Shoultz, 1982); Nancy Ward rose to become a widely respected voice for the rights of people with ID (Keith & Schalock, 2016a; Ward, 2000); and Ruth Sienkiewicz-Mercer, whose post-institutional advocacy led to improved lives for many, played a role in closure of the Belchertown State School (Sienkiewicz-Mercer & Kaplan, 1989).

Still other people with ID became known in terribly dramatic, unfortunate ways, as "freaks" in sideshows (Bogdan, 1988; Warren, 1851) or victims of the cruelty of the Holocaust (e.g., Zoech, 2003). And some were destined to become anonymous in death, buried beneath numbered brick markers (e.g., Dempsey, 2000) or in outcast cemeteries with no markers at all (Walsh, 2000). All of these people come to our attention because, whether in life or in death, they somehow stand out. Their stories, even when horrific, are out of the ordinary. Unfortunately, our written history is littered with too many of these sensational, negative stories, ranging from the brutal nature of institutions (Blatt & Kaplan, 1966; Wolfensberger, 1975) to victims of the eugenics movement (e.g., Goddard, 1912, 1914), denial of equal rights (Burgdorf & Burgdorf, 1975), and questions of who should live or die (e.g., Kuhse & Singer, 1985). But what, we might wonder, about the ordinary lives of ordinary people?

Ordinary People

We can sometimes feel bombarded by news of extraordinary people, whether extraordinary by virtue of celebrity, outrageous behavior, exceptional athletic skills, or enormous wealth. Such people generate media interest in a variety of ways, some of them admirable and others notorious. And, of course, there is also a cultural tendency to treat people with ID as somehow extraordinary, often in ways that paint them as inevitable sources of stress or pathology for their families (Dykens, 2005; Hodapp, 2002). Yet our daily lives are largely populated by ordinary people, and some of these ordinary people happen to be acquaintances with ID whose parents, despite a number of challenges, may be as well-adjusted as those of other children (Carr & O'Reilly, 2016), and whose families can experience a variety of positive aspects of having a family member with ID (Dykens, 2005; Floyd, Purcell, Richardson, & Kupersmidt, 2009).

Just as ordinary people may possess traits and behaviors that make them in some ways extraordinary friends or colleagues (e.g., Sack, 2015), so too might people with ID (Niemiec, Shogren, & Wehmeyer, 2017). Such strengths can include personal autonomy (Björnsdóttir, Stefánsdóttir, & Stefánsdóttir, 2015), communication, leisure activities, community participation, and interpersonal relationships, among others (Carter, Brock, & Trainor, 2012). In a study of 427 adolescents and young adults, Carter et al. (2015) found that parents were able to identify positive traits for every member of the sample, at every level of disability. Further, employers often describe people with ID as friendly and open (e.g., Andrews, 2005). Interestingly, the presence of a child with ID may also enhance the psychological growth of siblings (Findler & Vardi, 2009), and parents report many positive effects of parenting children with ID; among these are increased personal strength and confidence, enhanced appreciation of life, appreciation of children's accomplishments, and more meaningful relationships (Beighton & Wills, 2017).

Beyond the scholarly research on the subject, one need only read the moving accounts of parents (e.g., Brown, 2009) to grasp how important their children's legacies are to their families—a reality that transcends levels of disability. Thus, despite the anxiety and stress that can accompany parenting a child with ID, parents may value the opportunities for personal growth, pride, joy, and diversity of experience that come with the role (Lodewyks, 2015). And, like members of any other family, they have good reason to value and preserve the legacies of their children. They will remember the frustrations, successes, ups, downs, and love that characterize the memories that all of us hold for family and friends.

The Future: A New Way of Thinking About ID

People have long been inclined to organize and categorize things, including other people, into groups. Just as we group objects according to their salient traits (e.g., color, size, shape, function), so too do we group people, again according to obvious characteristics such as age, race, sex, nationality, or intelligence. Even when our categories are obsolete or essentially meaningless, we persist. For example, the concept of race is defined differently by different cultures and by researchers in different disciplines—it is essentially socially constructed (Eberhardt & Randall, 1997), with dubious biological bases (Zuckerman, 1990). Its boundaries are ambiguous and may vary according to social context (e.g., Davis, 1991). People of different cultures pay attention to different characteristics in grouping or categorizing (Ji, Zhang, & Nisbett, 2004), and their ways of classifying people can change over time. Thus, in American culture homosexuality was considered abnormal until the American Psychological Association and the American Psychiatric Association decided, in the 1970s, that it was not. However, it remained a disorder in China until well into the 21st century, when the Chinese Psychiatric Association changed its classification scheme.

In a similar vein, in 1973 large numbers of people who had carried the label "mental retardation" were no longer considered "retarded" due to a change in the classification criteria (from one to two standard deviations below average in measured IQ; Grossman, 1973; Trent, 1994). The people who were labeled did not change—but the characteristics defining their categories did. This is important, because our linguistic conceptualization of people can shape the ways we view and treat them (Lakoff & Johnson, 1980). Is ID a fixed entity in the real world, or is it a social construction, created in the minds of those in a position to label (Lea, 1988), or by environments ill-prepared to support the inclusion of people with individual needs (e.g., Rapley, 2004)? ID cannot, Burton Blatt (1999d) asserted, be encapsulated and portrayed by IQ or behavioral assessments, but is instead anchored to people, community, values, and hope.

Everyone a Unique Person

For two hundred years or more, Martha's Vineyard Island was home to a large proportion of people who were congenitally deaf. Yet, because everyone on the island spoke sign language, those with hearing impairments were not considered to have a disability (Groce, 1985). This is an extreme (but laudable) example of the power of social construction and the logical ultimate outcome of a supports paradigm. Because they had in place the personal supports characteristic of a truly adaptive environment, deaf people were able to function independently in their Martha's Vineyard communities. As Stancliffe, Arnold, and Riches (2016) observed, the supports paradigm is a broad concept, encompassing such aids as adaptive equipment, environmental design, and human helpers. Provision of significant personal supports is a step in the direction of making the *environment* exceptional (as Throne, 1972, advocated) instead of simply labeling the *person* as exceptional.

Provision of adequate supports has potential to dramatically change perceptions of disability and the legacies of people with ID. By providing a bridge between an individual's current status and a more desirable status, supports can connect what *is* to what *can be* (Arnold, Riches, Parmenter, & Stancliffe, 2009). On Martha's Vineyard, the support of a community fluent in sign language made it possible for everyone to be "normal," allowing one man, asked what townspeople had thought about the deaf residents, to say ". . . they didn't think anything about them, they were just like everyone else" (Groce, 1985, p. 2). Everyone, Groce reported, was remembered not for a disability, but as a unique individual.

Our Aim

In the remainder of this book, we intend to further examine the role of philosophy, psychology, medicine, and the broader community in creating cultural perceptions and legacies of people with ID that have often had their basis in stereotypes and misinformation. We will explore differing views of what it means to be human or who should live, and the profound implications of those views. Stereotypes and misconceptions were long maintained by isolated, segregated services, aided and abetted by the abuse and misuse of intelligence testing and labeling, and there have been movements to eradicate people with ID. We will see how cultures have dealt with the death and legacy of people with ID, who have sometimes been rendered nameless at the end of their lives.

We will then turn our attention to the future, further exploring how the social construction of ID, the quality-of-life revolution, and the supports movement can work toward a new moral community rooted in respect for the individual and individual rights, personal goals and choice, and broader cultural understanding. Families and friends of people with ID will help us to see the importance of their legacies, and people with ID will help us to know what is important in their lives and how they hope to be remembered. This, we believe, will take us another step closer to what we have called a new moral community (Keith & Keith, 2013) in which people are recognized for what they *can* do rather than what they *cannot* do (Bérubé, 2010). As geneticist Bruce Blumberg asserted, it is a mistake to consider people with ID as lesser. Instead, he said, "There is no lesser than. There's just different from. It isn't just great minds that matter. It's great spirits too" (Brown, 2009, p. 284). It is also courage, obstacles, heroism, development, love (Perske, 1980), and legacies.

Conclusion

A half century ago, it was not uncommon for infants who were presumed to have ID to be consigned to lives of institutional care, and to be seen as somehow less than human. Disability was considered a characteristic, a defect, of the individual, and in the eyes of the church and other institutions people with ID were "feeble-minded," or "idiots." Many of these "deviants" spent much of their lives far from family or friends, with little opportunity for interaction with people without disability. Negative attitudes toward people with ID are greater among people who do not have contact with them, despite the fact that ID is to a significant extent a social construct, its nature colored by those with the power to label it and give it definition.

Contemporary thought seeks to improve the lives of people with ID through provision of supports that allow for fuller participation in the mainstream of their communities. This approach to supporting people in their homes, schools, jobs, and social environments aims to get beyond the dehumanization that can accompany labeling and attitudes based on assumptions of individual defect. In the coming chapters we will discuss the circumstances that made clear the need for a new moral community, the philosophical and sociocultural perspectives that are making it possible, and the implications for the lives and legacies of people with ID.

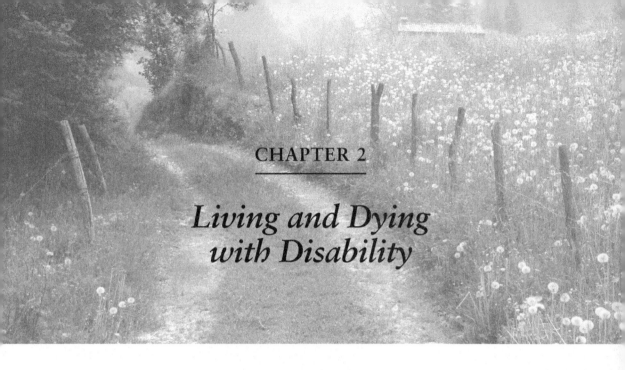

CHAPTER 2

Living and Dying with Disability

People with and without ID experience a wide range of feelings and attitudes about their lives. People with ID may have feelings of loss associated with the notion that they have somehow lost the opportunity for a normal life; anger and frustration due to the lack of understanding by others; or the emotions associated with the desire to know what (or who) is responsible for the difficulties of life with ID (Manners & Carruthers, 2006). At the same time, although they may be burdened with misconceptions and prejudice, people with ID can and do overcome adversity and live happy, productive lives (Fliesler, 2016). Their needs may be met in some areas but not in others (Bertoli et al., 2011), and daily life can be improved by the support afforded by appropriate training (Totsika, Toogood, Hastings, & McCarthy, 2010).

Despite the fact that many people with ID live satisfying lives, in discussions surrounding the question of who should live, philosophers have sometimes considered the life quality of parents and their children to be mutually exclusive (e.g., Singer, 1993). Aristotle (1988/350 BCE, p. 182) said ". . . let there be a law that no deformed child shall live." Other philosophers (e.g., Nussbaum, 2006, 2011) have taken a very different stance in advocating for the welfare of people with ID. This chapter will address some key questions about the implications, for people with ID, of philosophical views about who should live and who should decide. These questions may occur at birth or in infancy, and they can be critical later in life in relation to such issues as capital punishment, end-of-life care, and whether IQ alone can be the equivalent of a death sentence, in terms of treatments and care provided or denied.

This chapter will also explore the roles played by segregation and eugenics in shaping views of the lives and legacies of those with ID. It is little more than a century since public policies implemented at Ellis Island and elsewhere were used to label and reject immigrants presumed to have ID (e.g., Goddard, 1913a). The misuse of intelligence testing played a major role in this practice (Smith and Wehmeyer, 2012). These themes shape the remainder of this chapter.

Philosophy and a History of Debasement

Our idea of what it means to be human, who has rights, and who is part of our moral community have been questions central to Western philosophy for thousands of years. Such philosophical, or moral, systems have contributed to the dehumanization of people with ID. These ideas have ranged from Plato, who scaled human capacities in such a way that reason brings people closest to God-like perfection (Stainton 2001b), to the Enlightenment ideal of rationality as the apex of human singularity (e.g. Descartes, 1641/1952), to the dominant contemporary moral and political theories that assume that the capacity to intelligently explore duties or consequences is essential to moral goodness and full political inclusion (e.g. Rawls, 1999; Singer, 1993). Throughout the centuries, philosophy rests heavily on the idea that to be fully morally considerable, or even fully human, one must possess rationality and be of supposedly "normal" intelligence.

In ethics, the study which concerns the values and rightness or wrongness of human behavior, what it means to be morally considerable has largely been dependent on one's mental faculties. For example, Immanual Kant's (1785/1983) *deontology* (ethics based in moral obligation) calls for individuals to be fully in command of rational, rather than emotional, responses to moral quandaries. Such experiences as love, companionship, happiness, and empathy are, at most, positive side effects of moral decision-making. However, active moral engagement in Kantian deontology excludes people with disabilities because of their perceived inability to use reason to determine moral good. At best, someone with lesser perceived rationality might be a passive recipient of someone else's ethical activity, but not fully part of moral decision making. No amount of emotional intelligence, empathy, or even love is enough to merit one's status as a morally good person (i.e., having a good will) in Kant's deontology.

Some philosophers make a distinction between moral "agents" and moral "patients" (Regan, 2004). Moral agents are people who practice moral deliberation and are empowered to act on their moral thinking and values: "For Kant, moral agents exist only as ends in themselves; only those who are capable of applying abstract, impartial moral principles to their decision making share the right to be treated with respect" (Regan, 2004, p. xvii). Moral patients, on the other hand, may "have the same equal right to respectful treatment as do moral agents" (Regan, 2004, p. xvii), but because they are perceived by others as lacking a capacity for moral deliberation (via a traditional conception of rationality), their ability to contribute to moral decision making may not be cultivated or encouraged.

In the same vein as deontology, a utilitarian approach, while often promoting equal treatment, tends to limit moral agency to those who can use reason to calculate the best consequences. The utilitarian ethicist John Stuart Mill (2002/1861) famously said he would rather be "Socrates dissatisfied than a pig satisfied" because Socrates was rational (and the pig is not). If one is required to be rational in order to be moral, then only those without cognitive impairment could be moral agents. People with cognitive limitations might be classified as moral patients, acted upon by moral agents. In some cases, people who lack typical intellectual abilities may not even merit equality as moral patients when their interests seemingly conflict with others, as will be seen later in this chapter.

It should be noted that there are moral systems (such as care ethics, pragmatist ethics, Buddhist ethics, Confucian ethics, and even virtue theory as descended from Aristotle), which better integrate various qualities and abilities of all humans, including emotion and empathy (Keith & Keith, 2013). These theories tend to be grounded in relational and contextual views of the self. Some of these more relational theories will be explored later in a discussion of a new moral community that is more inclusive and diverse.

Out of Sight, Out of Mind

In the introduction to his *Idiocy: And its Treatment by the Physiological Method*, Édouard Séguin (1866/1907) extolled the virtue of an era in which "The right of all to education was acknowledged . . ." and "all nations encouraged the formation of schools for idiots . . ." (p. 9). Later in the same book, Séguin asserted that most "idiots" (people with ID) could be "relieved in a more or less complete measure of their disabilities by the physiological method of education" (p. 57). Building upon his belief that physical activity and education of the senses were essential to learning, Séguin (e.g., 1846) advocated for students to be actively engaged in the learning process. Early institutional superintendents shared Séguin's perspective, reporting successes in training and insisting that their facilities should not become asylums (Wolfensberger, 1975). For example, Samuel Gridley Howe wrote in 1852 about the value of the work done at one such institution, "One might as well weigh diamonds upon hayscales" (Richards, 1909, p. 219).

Segregation and the Rise of Institutions

However, it was not long until facilities that began as schools moved toward becoming asylums. These institutions grew in both number and size, and by the 1880s the prevalence of ID was believed to be growing and linked to other social problems. Between 1870 and 1880, the proportion of people identified as having ID more than doubled in every region of the U.S. (Gorwitz, 1974). Ironically, some of the perceived increase in prevalence may have been due to incentives received by census takers to report increased numbers of people with ID. The social construction of ID had begun (e.g., Trent, 1994), and the institutionalized population grew rapidly. By 1900, American institutions housed nearly 12,000 people with ID (Kuhlmann, 1940); the number in state institutions was 55,466 by 1926 (Lakin, 1979) and peaked at about 195,000 in 1967 (Lakin et al., 1989). In the state of New York alone, the number was about 16,000 by the start of World War II; and by the 1960s a single institution, the Willowbrook State School, housed more than 6,000 people (Goode, Hill, Reiss, & Bronston, 2013).

As institutions were growing in the late 19th century, so too were beliefs that ID was hereditary; that it was often the root of delinquency, crime, illegitimacy, and other presumed social and moral deficiencies; and that its prevalence was dramatically rising (Fernald, 1915; Wolfensberger, 1975). These views fueled enthusiasm for the continued development of segregated institutions as a protective measure for the broader society. Writing in 1909, J. M. Murdoch, superintendent of the State Institution for Feeble-Minded of

Western Pennsylvania, said this: "[C]areful diagnosis and quarantine, to the mental defective—quarantine not for forty days, but for life—will prevent more misery, pauperism, degeneracy, and crime and do more for the upbuilding of our race than any other measure within the power of man" (p. 64). Murdoch went on to suggest that those "found to be feeble-minded . . . should be set apart . . ." (p. 66). His colleague, New York commissioner Franklin Kirkbride (1909), wrote that " . . . it is essential that the feeble-minded and epileptic should be segregated . . ." (p. 87). Barr (1899) envisioned "colonies" that ". . . might be made almost self-supporting . . . scattered up and down throughout the land . . . " (p. 212). He argued that the time had come to "clear the way" for progress, and that turning these "irresponsibles" back into society would undo the good work of the institutions (p. 211).

Soon, Barr (1902b) would be advising his peers to abandon the hope of returning their charges to the world beyond the institution, thereby protecting society from this "pernicious element" (p. 6). Barr advocated for a national institution that, he believed, could be a self-sustaining "haven of irresponsibility" (p. 8). The movement toward total institutionalization was well underway (Trent, 1994), eventually culminating in long-term placements of individuals in facilities far removed from their families, and from which the most common form of egress was often death (e.g., Wolfensberger, 2002b). These were people who truly were out of sight, out of mind. For many of them, Blatt (1999a, p. 14) observed, their funerals came ". . . not with death but in life. For them, it is life that is the terrible avenger; it is life we mourn."

Immigration and the Eugenics Movement

The term "eugenics," coined in 1883 by Francis Galton (Aubert-Marston, 2009), came to mean the improvement of the population through controlled breeding. Galton advocated "positive eugenics," with the goal of fostering mentally and physically superior people. However, the other side of the eugenics coin, "negative eugenics," aimed to eliminate presumed inheritable, socially undesirable traits (Goode et al., 2013). Consistent with the aim of negative eugenics, Barr (1902a) likened the reproduction of those with mental deficiency to that of animals, lamenting that the reproduction of "irresponsible imbeciles" was not subject to the same restraints as that of "our flocks and herds and beasts of burden" (p. 163). A decade later, eight states had adopted laws authorizing or requiring surgical sterilization of certain classes of people, including people with ID, and thousands of sterilizations had been performed (Van Wagenen, 1914). Although the first sterilization law had been passed in 1907 in Indiana, California, having passed a law in 1909 providing for sterilization of "inmates" of state institutions, became a eugenics hotbed (Stern, 2005). By the late 1920s, California alone had sterilized about 6,000 people with ID (Wehmeyer, 2003). By the 1930s, a majority of American states and several Canadian provinces had adopted laws authorizing sterilization of people with ID (Spiro, 2009), and some remained in place well beyond the middle of the 20th century (e.g., Harper, 2002; Wolfensberger, 2002b).

Barr (1899) and Murdoch (1909), like other leaders of their time, wanted to isolate people with ID not only to prevent their expected criminal or delinquent behavior, but also to ensure that they did not reproduce. Contemporary psychologist Henry Goddard (1912, 1913a, 1914), also believed that mental deficiency was indeed hereditary. In his infamous genealogy report of the spurious Kallikak family, Goddard (1912) purported to show that differences between branches of the family tree, whether descended from a "feeble-minded tavern girl" or a Quaker woman from a "good family," were inherited. In more recent times, of course, Goddard's analysis has been discredited (e.g., Elks, 2005; Gould, 1981; Greenwood, 2009), but his influence was strong. In response to heavy immigration to the United States, Congress had enacted legislation to restrict the immigration of those with ID or mental illness (referred to as"idiots" and "lunatics"; Reed, 1913). Goddard embarked upon an effort to screen immigrants arriving at Ellis Island. Based upon their presumed "ability" to detect potential mental deficiency via someone's appearance, Goddard and his assistants selected people for screening (Hunt, 1994). Goddard approached the work with enthusiasm, and without taking language and culture into account in testing people, he labeled nearly 80 percent of some groups (e.g., Italians, Jews, Hungarians, Russians) "mentally deficient" (Goddard, 1917). Accordingly, deportations of these groups increased markedly in 1913 and 1914 (Hunt, 1994). Overall, Goddard believed that nearly half of all immigrants were "mentally deficient."

Goddard was not alone in his beliefs about the hereditary nature of intelligence and its prevalence in various ethnic groups. Lewis Terman (1916), one of the most prominent psychologists of the early 20th century, strongly believed that some racial and ethnic groups (notably "Negroes," Mexicans, and Spanish-Indian people of the American Southwest) were inherently intellectually inferior. Terman also thought that ". . . from a eugenic point of view they present a grave problem because of their unusually prolific breeding" (p. 92). Views such as these contributed not only to segregation of people with ID, but also to their sterilization. Goddard (1913b), who believed all cases of ID to be hereditary, asserted that a woman with ID should never become a mother.

From Galton's advocacy of selective breeding in his 1869 book *Hereditary Genius*, to Supreme Court Justice Oliver Wendell Holmes's misguided assertion that "Three generations of imbeciles are enough" (Buck v. Bell, 1927), to the mandatory sterilization laws of the 20th century, the legacy of the eugenics movement is a sad commentary on the history of treatment of people with ID. And although the movement was largely discredited because of the Nazi atrocities, in the years leading up to World War II American organizations (e.g., Rockefeller Foundation, Carnegie Institution, IBM) had cooperated with German researchers in providing funding and technical support. Furthermore, in the United States, the *Journal of the American Medical Association* reported the work of German eugenicist Ernst Rübin (Citizens Commission on Human Rights, 2018), the *Eugenical News* published work lauding Adolf Hitler's views on eugenics, and in 1932 New York City hosted the International Congress of Eugenics (Black, 2012). The Nazi party was a firm believer in the value of eugenics, which played a role, of course, in sterilization and in the eventual extermination of thousands of people.

The Ethics of Decision Making for Others

Our recorded history contains many examples in which people make decisions concerning the life, education, healthcare, quality of life, and end of life of people with ID. All of these decisions regarding education, healthcare, job training, or access to housing and more, are fundamental to the way of life of all people, including those with ID. The ways such life-and-death decisions are made is important, and perhaps the most fundamental question of all is who should make these decisions.

Infants with Disabilities

Many perspectives in ethics, no matter how much they emphasize diversity and equality, have disturbing roots in categorizing people by their capacity to reason. At best, most philosophers and ethicists have viewed people with disabilities as moral patients, to be cared for, but not to be involved in ethical decision making, even when it concerns their own interests. An additional consequence of such a strong focus on reason and traditional intelligence is the assumption that people with ID have a lower quality of life than their non-disabled peers, which leads many people to believe that life with ID is not a life worth living.

A perspective that seeks to measure the quality of one person's life in comparison to an idealized version of a life most certainly influences decisions relating to terminating pregnancies (Stangle, 2010), euthanizing infants, and ending the lives of older children with disabilities (Soy, 2018). Such disregard for diverse ways of being abled has led to selective abortion as a widely acceptable response to disability (Stangle, 2010), sometimes even when it is clear that the disability in question may not diminish quality of life as severely as parents and doctors expect. Some ethicists even call for infant euthanasia as a morally appropriate response to babies born with disabilities (Kuhse & Singer, 1985; Smoker, 2003), a practice that is increasingly legally permissible (Nuwer, 2014; Voultsos & Chatzinikolaou, 2014). Cultural beliefs about the social burden of having to support individuals with disabilities and questions about the potential for positive quality of life have caused doctors, philosophers, and families to wonder whether infants with disabilities should live or die, and there are even some places (e.g., Kenya, Bolivia) where, due to cultural or political beliefs, parents are pressured to kill children with disabilities (de Hilari, Condori, & Dearden, 2009; Soy, 2018).

The False Dichotomy: Individual Quality of Life Versus Family Quality of Life

Greater access to legal means of euthanasia does not necessarily denote greater ease in evaluating quality of life, no matter the ethical approach one employs (Jotkowitz & Glick, 2006; Kon 2008; Voultsos & Chatzinikolaou, 2014). In 1985, Helga Kuhse and Peter Singer famously wrote in their book *Should the Baby Live,* that even when it is determined that a child with a disability has the potential ability to enjoy a positive quality of life, prolonging the child's existence may not be in the family's best interest; therefore, they asked, "Which should we choose: the family or the child?" While Kuhse and Singer calculated children's and families' interests, sometimes seemingly in opposition, the perception of those interests is only as good as the information families and doctors have, and their willingness to imagine a variety of ways of being in the world. Some critics have claimed that Kuhse and Singer posed a false dilemma by failing to consider whether, with different supports in place, both the child's and the family's quality of life could be improved (e.g., Kittay, 2010), or that some people with ID might actually enjoy a much better quality of life than many typically abled people (Wong, 2000). Alexander Kon (2008) noted that

> many people who believe that they would never want to live with serious disability (e.g., quadriplegia) later believe that their life is fulfilling and very much worth living when faced with the reality of life with disability. Further, studies have demonstrated that even close family members and spouses are poor judges of the end of life choices of patients (p. 28).

This inability to take the perspective of another person is more confounding when attempting to imagine future quality of life from an infant's perspective. Micah Hester (2010) suggested that rather than alleviating suffering via the irreversible act of euthanasia, we put more resources into palliative care which honors the fact that we cannot fully know what is best for the present or future well-being of an infant and "palliative care allows for flexibility in decision making" (p. 150).

As Hester (2001) reported, we invariably impose our own biases about whether life with disability is worth living when making decisions about selective abortion or euthanasia. This view that no one would want to live such a life, Hester noted, is reasonably troubling to people living with disabilities. Likewise, Rebecca Stangl (2010) argued that selective termination (abortion) in substitutionary cases (i.e., terminating pregnancy in the case of disability in order to allow for the birth of a "healthy" baby later) is clearly disrespectful to people with disabilities.

Intellectual Disability and the Death Penalty

As adults, people with ID have also been vulnerable to life-threatening policies and practices. One such threat has been capital punishment. The death penalty has long existed within the legal frameworks of many nations. Capital punishment arrived in North America with early colonists, and there were numerous executions during the 17th century. Eventually, states adopted the death penalty and, despite various efforts to abolish it, by the end of the 19th century most states retained capital punishment (Death Penalty Information Center, 2018).

People with ID are generally law-abiding citizens, but when they do have contact with the criminal justice system, they can be vulnerable and may be susceptible to victimization (e.g., Jones, 2007). In recent times, the use by states of the death penalty has significantly declined; however, of those who were executed, like those involved with the criminal justice system more broadly (Polloway, Patton, & Smith, 2015), a disproportionate number are people with ID (Fair Punishment Project, 2016).

After lagging behind other Western countries, the United States, by virtue of the 2002 Supreme Court ruling in *Atkins v. Virginia*, outlawed the death penalty for people with ID (French, 2005). In the view of the Court, the death penalty violated the Eighth Amendment prohibition of cruel and unusual punishment. Just 13 years earlier, however, the Court had declined to prohibit the death penalty for a man with ID in *Penry v. Lynaugh*, holding that there was no national legislative consensus against execution (Libell, 2007). This was true despite poll data suggesting that two-thirds of Americans opposed the execution of people with ID (Keyes & Edwards, 1997). And, in deciding the *Atkins* case, the Court elected not to define "mental retardation," instead leaving that task to the individual states—a circumstance that provided a prohibition on execution without also providing procedural guidelines to state courts (e.g., Appelbaum, 2009; Widroff & Watson, 2008). Thus, the Supreme Court decided that people with ID should not be executed, but left states to decide who is in fact a person with ID. One result was an over-reliance on intelligence test scores (Foley, 2015), even though the levels of scores denoting ID have changed over time (e.g., Beirne-Smith, Patton, & Ittenbach, 1994) and psychologists may disagree about proper reporting and interpretation of IQ scores (see, e.g., Hagan, Drogin, & Guilmette, 2010).

Sadly, in the face of potential vulnerability to suggestion or coercion in dealings with law enforcement (Salekin & Everington, 2015), false confessions (Perske, 2008), and a long history of misunderstanding, stereotyping, and neglect by the courts, the legacy of some people with ID is distorted or forgotten. Little attention may be paid to the cultural background of defendants with ID (Ruth, 2015), jurors may sometimes be confused about the relevance of ID (Keyes & Edwards, 1997), and exoneration, if it comes at all, may come long after the execution of people who, in addition to having ID, may never have violated any law (e.g., Greenspan, 2011). And, of course, we will never know how many people with ID were tried, convicted, and executed without adequate evaluation or legal representation, and with no recognition of their disability. Lost to history, they have too often been name-less in death.

Conclusion

This chapter examined perspectives on the human condition and how people with ID have been dehumanized historically. Such treatment of people with ID has powerful implications, not only for the individuals themselves, but for the rest of the culture as well. If it is true, as many writers and leaders have asserted, that we should judge a civilization by its treatment of its most vul-nerable citizens, it is in the interest of all citizens to ensure just and humane policies and practices for people with ID.

Segregation, misuse of IQ testing and labeling, and mistaken assump-tions about the nature and quality of life experienced by people with ID have brought needless grief to many families and individuals who have had important life decisions made for them, including decisions that have literally involved matters of life and death, from (or before) the moment of birth to end-of-life decisions. The next chapter will address how people with ID die and how their passing is noted.

CHAPTER 3

Nameless in Death

In recent years in the United States, people with ID have been increasingly seen as having the right to a good quality of life, and to the same civil rights as people without disabilities (Todd & Read, 2009). However, and for too many years, people with ID were consigned to isolated, unmarked cemeteries or in graves elsewhere (such as on the grounds of institutions) that did not carry their names. An additional measure of the perceived worth of people with ID can be found in the practices and perspectives that attend their deaths.

Prominent philosophers and biologists sometimes argue that allowing infants with disability to die may be the most nearly ethical course; hospitals may enforce policies and implement procedures inconsistent with the cultural traditions of some dying patients; some cultures for many years consigned people with disability to isolated, unmarked cemeteries; and many institutions purporting to serve the needs of people with ID long maintained cemeteries in which graves did not carry the names of the people buried there.

Many people with ID live satisfying lives and are in many cases inspiring examples for their families and friends. Yet too many continue to live and die as outsiders, unknown or unaccepted in their communities. This chapter will discuss some of the ways that people with ID have been treated in death, and the meanings ascribed to their lives by their communities.

Tombs of the Unknown

The Holocaust and Deaths of People With ID

Between 1934 and 1939, more than 300,000 Germans were sterilized, particularly those with mental or physical disability, under the Law for the Prevention of Progeny with Hereditary Diseases (Grue, 2009; Holocaust Educational Trust, n.d.). Then, in1939, the Reich Committee for the Scientific Registration of Severe Hereditary Ailments (Reich Committee) decreed that all "malformed" newborns and young children be registered. Among those subject to this order were children with Down syndrome, hydrocephaly, microcephaly, cerebral palsy, and other neurological disorders. Their records were reviewed in Berlin by a medical panel who, without so much as seeing the children, marked each file, indicating whether the child should die or live. Those chosen for death were taken to hospitals, to children's killing wards, usually without parental consent. Parents later received form letters notifying them of their child's death. In this way, thousands of children died in anonymity, far from home and family (Evans, 2004).

The Reich Committee existed only on paper; it was a phony front for the activities of the Chancellery of the Führer and the decree requiring registration of children was disguised as a request for scientific information (Friedlander, 1995). Children in the killing wards died of starvation or lethal doses of drugs (DiConsiglio, 2015), and Nazi physicians insisted that children and their families had been helped, in view of fact that (in the doctors' judgment) the children could never become human (Parent & Shevell, 1998). The Reich Committee asked parents or welfare agencies to pay for the children's "treatment" (Friedlander, 1995) and Nazi doctors profited by selling children's organs to universities, laboratories, and corporations (Evans, 2004).

Awful as it was, the size of the killing program for children paled in comparison to the T4 program (named for its headquarters at Tiergartenstrasse 4 in Berlin), authorized by Hitler late in 1939 to grant a "mercy death" to people with diseases considered incurable. Hitler was encouraged by the progress of the children's killing program, and determined to exterminate adults with disabilities. The Reich Committee required that institutions report information on patients, including ID (Friedlander, 1995). Then, in killing centers at Bernburg, Brandenburg, Grafeneck, Hadamar, Hartheim, and Sonnenstein, the Nazis murdered at least 100,000 people with disabilities (Evans, 2004).

People arriving at the killing centers were reduced to ashes within 24 hours, their cremated remains randomly placed into urns. Those families who were able to acquire such an urn did not know that the remains they received were not those of their loved one—that they had simply come from a pile of ash created by mass cremation (Friedlander, 1995). Like children in the pediatric killing centers, adults with disability also died unknown and isolated from family.

However, the perception of people with ID as a social menace, subject first to sterilization and then euthanasia, was not strictly a Nazi view. Polls conducted in the late 1930s showed that nearly half of American respondents supported the euthanasia of babies with disabilities (Noack & Fangeroa, 2007; Yount, 2000). And the practice of euthanasia, or mercy killing, is not a thing of the past, unfortunately. The practice continues, albeit on a far smaller scale. For example, in the Netherlands doctors may assist in ending the life of people enduring "unbearable suffering." About 7,000 people were euthanized in 2017 (Boffey, 2018). Of those, a significant number were newborns, and although the annual number of newborns with disability euthanized is much smaller than in earlier times—estimates range from 15 or 20 (Verhagen & Sauer, 2005) to 100 (Griffiths, Weyers, & Adams, 2008)—the issue remains very much alive.

Burials at Institutional Cemeteries

As late as the mid-20th century, family members of people with ID encountered a near-total lack of community supports (e.g., Ferdinand & Marcus, 2002). In 1965 more than 164,000 Americans with ID lived in public institutions (Butterfield, 1969) that housed, on average, more than 1,500 people each. Many more lived in private institutions, which had grown dramatically in number earlier in the 20th century (Trent, 1994). And, in the 1950s and early 1960s, as many as a third of new institutional admissions were people with ID who had milder levels of impairment (Lakin, 1979)—people who would have been capable of productive work and living in the community, with appropriate training and support (Menolascino, 1977).

Institutions were often built in isolated locations, sometimes on land donated by communities hoping to attract new job opportunities (Wolfensberger, 1975). For example, the institution that would become Syracuse (NY) State School had its beginning on 10 acres of land offered by the city of

Syracuse (Goode, Hill, Reiss, & Bronston, 2013). Some early superintendents had romantic notions of self-sustaining farm communities or "colonies," with sufficient farm land to support dairies, gardens, crop land, and orchards—places that would be, according to one early authority, "village(s) of the simple" (Johnson, 1899, p. 472). In view of the locations of many institutions, it should not be surprising that many individuals had little contact with their families (Trent, 1994; Wolfensberger, 2002) or that staff were as isolated as the institutional residents (Wolfensberger, 1975).

The institutions grew steadily until the 1960s (Lakin, 1979), and with dramatic growth in size came increased potential for dehumanizing treatment of the people living in them. The increased potential for dehumanization was compounded by the attitudes perpetuated in the demeaning names of the facilities, many of which used the terms "feeble-minded," "idiots," or "imbecile." Overcrowding became common, fences and barbed wire were in evidence, and living areas sometimes had locked doors and bars on windows (e.g., Blatt & Kaplan, 1966). Death in some facilities must surely have brought relief, even if it meant dying alone, without family or friends.

Dying in institutions has sometimes meant that people became literally nameless in death. For example, at the Eastern State Hospital cemetery in Kentucky, established early in the 19th century, only three graves (of a number estimated to be at least 4,000–5,000) have headstones (Find a Grave, 2018). The location of these graves was unknown for many years, until they were discovered in 1984 by the city of Lexington (Abandoned, 2018). Recently in Mississippi construction at the university's medical center campus led to discovery of an estimated 7,000 graves from an institution dating from 1855 (Dockrill, 2017).

In Minnesota, nearly 13,000 residents of state facilities serving a variety of vulnerable people, including those with ID, were buried in unmarked graves (Boyd, 2007). In other states, institutions for people with ID marked graves with numbers (but not names), and kept a record of the names in a separate place. This strategy was used in Massachusetts (Sullivan, 2015), Virginia (Smith, 1995), and Nebraska where, in the words of the Center for Disability Rights, Law and Advocacy (2007, p. 9) ". . . they became forgotten with their life stories of hope, despair, love, and anguish buried under numbered tombstones . . . nameless in death."

Burial of the Unclaimed

Advocates in a number of states have undertaken efforts to mark or to honor the burial sites of people with ID. This is true in Massachusetts (Sullivan, 2015), Wisconsin, Georgia, South Carolina, Ohio, New York, and Minnesota (Antlfinger, 2015), among others. However, in some circumstances state authorities may, even today, bury individuals with ID in unmarked graves (e.g., Reyes, 2017). State authorities make such arrangements for paupers and others who are unidentified.

The practice of burying some groups of social outsiders in isolated places is not of recent origin. Since at least the 17th century, so-called children's burial grounds in Ireland have been the sites of graves of a number of outcast groups, including people with ID (Murphy, 2011; Nolan, 2006). The origins of this practice likely lay in the church, arising from the view that these groups, like unbaptized children, represented "others," whose remains should be separated from those of people buried in consecrated ground, and the unmarked burial grounds were called killeens (*cillíní* in Irish; Garattini, 2007). *Cillíní* were often placed in marginal locations (Finlay, 2000), so that "even in death, these nameless individuals earned no more than a place apart from the established community" (Walsh, 2000, p. 315). Although some *cillíní* were in use as recently as the middle of the 20th century (Aldridge, 1969), hundreds remain unknown to contemporary citizens (e.g., Murphy, 2011; O'Sullivan & Sheehan, 1996). Despite the marginalization, by the church and proper society, of those interred in *cillíní*, they were sacred places for families, and today communities and advocates are working together to preserve their legacies (e.g., Hall, 2014).

The cemetery at the institution for people with ID at Leyme, in France, opened around 1835 with spaces for 1,000 graves. When these were filled (in 1923 and again in 1944), the remains were exhumed and moved to another plot, making way for more bodies. The graves are marked with identical crosses (without regard for religion of the deceased), only one bearing a name, and two carrying dates of birth and death; a register holds information about the deceased (Védie & Breathnach, 2005). In England, the cemetery at the former Calderstones Hospital, an institution for people with ID, was sold to private developers and has changed hands multiple times (Magee,

2012). Gravestones have been removed, and former residents have protested further development that they fear will disturb the graves of friends buried at Calderstones (Norris, 2018).

Conceptualizing Death Across Cultures

Although the definition of death might seem to be an uncomplicated matter, some, even within the medical community, do not agree on the criteria to use to determine death. For example, death could be defined by the cessation of heart and lung functions, or death could be determined by neurological criteria (President's Council on Bioethics, 2008). Brain death might mean cessation of activity in the cortex, which is the location of the higher-level functions. Or brain death might mean that activity has ceased in both the cortex and in the brainstem, where such basic functions as breathing and heartbeat are controlled (Gire, 2014). Defining death in terms of such criteria is of course an aspect of the Western biomedical approach, and inevitably leads to difficult ethical decisions in the case of individuals who, due to head injury, congenital conditions, or other causes, may have little likelihood of gaining or resuming consciousness.

Just as researchers working across cultures have examined issues related to the quality of life with ID (e.g., Keith & Schalock, 2016), so too have they discussed the role of culture in perceptions of people with disability as they approach death, when a diminished sense of personhood associated with disability can be especially acute (Luborsky, 1994). They have found that physicians may fail to resuscitate people with ID "because" of their disability (Bingham, 2013). Families of patients with ID in the United Kingdom may believe that medical personnel do not adequately listen to or communicate with them, and research has shown that seriously ill people with ID some-times receive less effective medical care and thus die prematurely at significantly higher rates than other people (Heslop et al., 2013). Other research has found that people with ID in Australia and the United States tend to have poor hospital experiences (Ailey, Brown, & Ridge, 2017; Iacono et al., 2014), and they may not be taken seriously if physicians attribute potentially important symptoms to their ID (Perry, 2018).

Cultural and spiritual beliefs, as well as language barriers, may affect understanding of diagnosis and treatment, and attitudes toward people with ID differ across cultures (Scior, Kan, McLoughlin, & Sheridan, 2010).

Similarly, the rituals associated with death also vary across cultures, along such dimensions as outward expression of grief, preference for cremation or burial, keeping the corpse at home (or not) until the funeral, dressing the body, receiving guests during a mourning period, or positioning the body to face a holy site (Lobar, Youngblut, & Brooten, 2006). Most people in Western cultures go to a hospital to die, even though death may not be mentioned, and patients may believe that medical science will overcome the prospect of death (Parkes, Laungani, & Young, 1997).

Unfortunately, when medical care providers assume dominance, they can be ethnocentric and may impede communication, failing to grasp cultural views that might be important to the well-being and acceptance of the patient (and family), especially in the face of death (Putsch & Joyce, 1990). Some cultural groups may arrange large gatherings of people to show respect and support for a family member dying or close to death (e.g., Moore, 2015; Northern Sydney Local Health District, 2015). At the time of death, as in life, it is critical that professionals have the attitudes, skills, and knowledge— the cultural competence—to meet the needs of people from diverse cultures (Elphinstone, 2018; Lonner, 2013).

People with and without ID respond to the illness and death of others in diverse ways. Some people are resilient and easily able to understand the death of a loved one, and others will need specific supports. For those who need supports, caregivers will need a structured plan for helping them to adapt after receiving bad news (Tuffrey-Wigne, 2013). The parent of a child with severe ID suggested that many people with ID may understand more than we realize about issues of death and dying (Kittay, 2011).

Despite cultural differences in perceptions and observance of death, the experience of death cuts across all boundaries. Todd and Read (2009) have raised important questions that are concerned with how the person with ID is understood after their death. Among these are the following: What identity do people with ID have after their death? What becomes of a person's ID after death—is it a part of their legacy? Is ID useful only to categorize the individual in life? If the influence of ID is important in life, why do we not ask what difference it makes in death? How are people with ID remembered? How can they exert influence over the way they are remembered? How can death illuminate the social worth and value of people with ID? Although there may not be clear answers to these questions, people with ID have much to say about death, and talking about the link between ID, death, and how they wish to be remembered can help them to clarify what it means to have ID (Todd & Read, 2009). Too often, as Todd and Read suggested, death may be a forgotten aspect of life.

Conclusion

How people are treated in death reflects how they are viewed in life. We see this in the extermination of devalued groups in the Holocaust, and in the quality of life experienced by people with ID in large institutions, followed by burial in unmarked graves far from family and home.

Despite cultural variations in views of death and the value of people with ID, the experience of death is universal, and care providers who support people as they or their loved ones die with ID need the skills and under-standing—the cultural competence—to provide quality care at the end of life. Families, friends, and supporters of people with ID need to face the questions raised by death—questions of identity, personal value, and legacy. The next chapter explores these questions in the context of the development of a moral community in which all people have value and many people with ID can take a more active role in moral decision making about their own lives.

CHAPTER 4

A New Moral Community

The idea of disability as a social construction is not new, although much of the historical literature of the ID field has focused, over many years, on the biomedical aspects of disability as a trait of the person. This focus on disorders, syndromes, defects, and handicaps as personal characteristics has sometimes produced conflict between those advocating treatment-based approaches and those calling for supported community life in settings as close as possible to those of people without disabilities. For some philosophers, this conflict has also resulted in a dilemma: Are there those whose quality of life, or whose capacity for reason, are so deficient that death might be better than the life they are consigned to live? For others, disability draws forth a greater capacity for empathy, love, and care than they might otherwise have known.

In this chapter we review the possibilities for differing ethical perspectives on the qualities involved in being human. We discuss the ways we may become morally engaged with people with ID, and how the choices we make may change lives—for those with ID and for those without. Poet John Donne (1829) wrote, "No man is an island entire of itself." We are all, with or without disability, connected. It behooves us then, to reflect on our common humanity and to support the ability of individuals with ID to speak for themselves and to become fully participating members of the community.

The Social Construct of Disability

The range of medical conditions and disorders long associated with ID comprises a lengthy, daunting list (see, e.g., Menolascino & Egger, 1978). Jenkins (1998), however, argued that such labels as "mental retardation" are not natural or real, except as classifications of Western medicine and psychology—that is, that they are cultural constructs that may lack relevance in many local settings around the world. Rapley (2004, p. 43) suggested this appropriation of terms like "disorder," "sign," "symptom," and "syndrome," while often allowing misuse of the terms, facilitates professional control over people so labeled. Unfortunately, diagnosis of disability in this way often conveys the message that people with disabilities and their families face disappointment and distress, as well, perhaps, as grief and suffering (Reinders, 2000).

Labeling of the condition now known as ID dates from at least as early as 1324, in the statute *De Praerogative Regis* ("of the king's prerogative"; Lunacy and Idiocy, 1951). Through the centuries, a wide variety of terms now considered very offensive have been used to label people with ID, culminating in the long use of "mental retardation" (Wolfensberger, 2002a), and the official advent in the 21st century of "intellectual disability" (Schalock et al., 2007), and a multi-dimensional classification scheme (Schalock et al., 2010).

An interesting, and important, aspect of the changing labels attached to people with ID is the fact that, as the various descriptions of people change, the people do not. Yet changing labels may affect people's lives in important ways. Thus, as we saw in Chapter 1, when the American classification system changed the IQ level used to denote mental retardation (Grossman, 1973), a large number of people were no longer "retarded," despite the fact that the individuals themselves had not changed. The labels and the classifications we invent to characterize people become a part of the narrative of their lives, their stories. And stories—the language we use to describe people's lives—have the power to effect profound changes, for better or worse, in their lives (e.g., Blatt, 1999b). As Blatt noted, sometimes ID is "an untrue and unnecessary story about a large group of people" (p.86). In a sense, people have a disability because someone, or some authority, says they do.

Yet, while some authors (e.g., Silvers, Waserman, & Mahowald, 1998) have suggested that the biomedical model of disability discounts the role of social influences in the lives of people with disability, it seems clear that the relation between physical embodiment (biology, neurology, genetics, physical nature) and the social (family, community, culture) is fundamental to understanding people, their needs, and their quality of life. A social constructionist view, then, does not deny the reality of disability, but at the same time recognizes the responsibility of society to provide the services and supports necessary to meet individual needs (Oliver, 1996). It prompts us to say that disability lies as much with society as with the individual. Chapter 5 will explore the nature and role of supports in the new moral community. The remainder of this chapter will discuss our ethical traditions to determine whether a social view of ethics can result in a community more likely to engage all of its members.

Moral Engagement: Implications for Intellectual Disability

Moral engagement connotes the ability to commit to ethical behavior toward others and the courage to engage in such behavior. It requires a community of others who encourage and accept one's deliberations and decisions. As discussed in Chapter 2, the Western ethical tradition largely discounted the capacity of moral reasoning by people with ID. When ethicists address it, it is often in developing arguments from marginal cases for the benefit of other groups. For example, one of Peter Singer's (2009, 2010) central arguments in favor of animal rights exploits humans with disabilities in a marginal case argument against "speciesism." Singer argued that it would be speciesist (in the same vein as racist or sexist) for us to abuse or neglect nonhuman animals if we were not willing to do such things to humans whom Singer views as having similar intellectual capacities. For example, Singer might say, if we are willing to conduct painful or life-threatening tests on nonhuman animals, such as chimpanzees or dogs, we should be willing to conduct the same tests on humans with intellectual disability with a high level of impairment. If not, we are speciesist and unethical. Of course, Singer doesn't think we should conduct painful or dangerous tests on people with disabilities—that is just part of his argument calling attention to what he views as the unethical treatment of nonhuman animals. His use of people with disabilities, however, as part of his marginal case argument, might marginalize people with ID even more. Marginal case theories are widely used, especially in animal rights literature (Carlson, 2009), which not only alienates and disrespects real human beings in thought experiments about causing suffering to people with disabilities or to animals, but also assumes that all people with disabilities, in their sameness, should, perhaps, be marginalized. As Licia Carlson (2009) noted, "Here again we find that intellectual disability is assumed to be a self-evident category of individuals about whom philosophical analogies and comparisons can be made" (p. 11). As moral patients, people are acted upon, rather than active members of a moral community. All of this kind of discussion to the effect that people with ID are morally equivalent to animals is dehumanizing, and extremely offensive.

Many critics of Singer and other philosophers who use marginal case arguments suggest that using humans with disabilities to make arguments about the ethical treatment of animals goes too far in equating the two groups. Such arguments do not take into consideration the unique experience of humans, with their family connections, friendships, and their ability to take an active role in decision making with the appropriate supports. The late Harriet Johnson (2003) responded to Singer's argument: "because I am still seeking acceptance of my humanity, Singer's call to get past species seems a luxury way beyond my reach." Kittay (2010) suggested that ethicists like Singer also are missing the important experience of others who care for and about people with disabilities, seeing their value and worth. Ian Brown (2009) similarly wrote about how much he has grown morally as the father of a child with ID. A model of disability that respects individuals and recognizes and honors the social context of human relationships, and ethical theories that support networks of care rather than logical calculation or marginal cases, are more likely to result in a more expansive community that contributes to the moral growth of all its members, rather than just those with a traditionally delineated rationality.

Ways of caring for people with disabilities are also dependent on our cultural view of individual interests and who should, and can, be involved in making moral decisions. In 2006, the balance of interests was put to the test in the case of Ashley X, known for the "Ashley Treatment." In this case, Ashley was a six-year-old girl with severe ID and a number of physical disabilities whose parents made the decision to use hormones and surgery to attenuate her growth in order to keep her physically small and prevent puberty through a combination of hormones and invasive procedures, such as a hysterectomy and breast bud removal. Ashley's parents stated that their purpose was to prevent her from being the victim of sexual abuse as she grew, to avoid uncomfortable menstruation, and to keep her small enough that her family could continue to care for her at home as long as possible (Gunther & Diekema, 2006). The Ashley Treatment has since been used on other children in similar circumstances (Greig, 2015).

Singer, a proponent of the Ashley Treatment, noted that the treatment caused Ashley's body to match her supposed "mental age," keeping her child-sized and allowing her parents to include her in more activities because she was easier to carry (2007). Other parents who have chosen the Ashley Treatment for their children likewise believe they are acting in their children's best interests by making it more likely that they can stay at home (Field, 2016). Critics (e.g., Harnacke, 2016) claim that the Ashley Treatment discounts the potential for adults with disabilities to one day contribute to decisions about their care, in violation of both ethical and legal standards (American Association on Intellectual and Developmental Disabilities, 2012b). They also claim that families are more likely prioritizing their own interests (to keep children baby-like and manageable) above those of their children. As is explored in this chapter, both of these views assume that interests are primarily individualized, and not tangled up together, and that there are no solutions in the wider social context that would avoid seemingly conflicting issues. For example, a Hastings Center working group (Wilfond et. al., 2010) noted that Ashley's parents faced a dilemma. Her potential difficulties (abuse and neglect in case it became impossible for her family to care for her at home) were largely socially constructed and she and her family thus needed more social resources to overcome them. But those resources were lacking, so a medical fix seemed like a viable option. Surgery and hormones fit the medical model of disability; greater resources and understanding in the family and community might have been possible under the social model. Karrie Shogren, co-director of the Kansas University Center on Developmental Disabilities, said "One of my major concerns . . . is that places where this is being done might tend to be places that don't have strong disability affiliations or support" (Field, 2016). Kittay (2011) argued that the views of the parents in wishing to keep children with ID more child-like discounts the potential growth of their minds and relationships, as well as their bodies: To have the mind of a baby and the capacities of a baby are not the same thing, for the disabled person may well have an understanding and a set of emotional responses that far exceed her capacity to act. The brain may be impaired, but it is not frozen. Synapses continue to be formed as they do in all brains.

The Ashley Treatment and the consequences of growth attenuation as children grow to adulthood seem unlikely to contribute to the cultural changes essential to a more inclusive moral community. And Kittay (2011, p. 627) wrote

> ... still more important is the environment of inclusion: of welcoming many sorts of bodies and minds, seeing the world as enriched by this diversity, and embracing the possibilities as well as the challenges presented by those who diverge from the norm.

What foundation in our ideals and moral theories can we find to support diverse and equitable communities that support people of all abilities in meeting their needs, listening to their voices, and appreciating their contributions? Jason Greig (2015), with a religious twist on the social model of disability, wrote "Recognizing Ashley as a gift worth welcoming as she is, rather than as a dilemma requiring surgical intervention is a compelling alternative to the medical model of disability that frames Ashley as object and perpetual child" (p. 44).

Foundations of a New Moral Community

The Social Context for Morality

Kuhse and Singer (1985), when asking whether a disabled baby's or her parents' interests are more important, assumed that those interests are easily separable. Philosophic views of people as essentially intelligent, rational decision makers assume selves, even those of parents and children, in isolation. However, many philosophies posit a human self as essentially social, whose interests are not easily separable from those of others, and which blurs the lines between moral patients and moral agents, or between parents and children: "The well-being of a child, assuming a loving family, is critical to the well-being of parents and siblings, just as their well-being is crucial to that of the child" (Kittay, 2011, p. 615). We believe some of these philosophic foundations are essential to developing a morally empowering view of people with disabilities.

For example, American pragmatist moral theory starts with the idea that the person is, from birth, a social creature. George Herbert Mead's (1934) social behaviorism, influenced by Wilhelm Wundt, posits the self as emerging from the social fold of family relationships: "The self is something which has a development; it is not initially there, at birth, but arises in the process of social experience and activity, that is, develops in the given individual as a result of his relations to that process as a whole and to other individuals within that process" (p. 135).

Mead's colleague John Dewey (1927/1988), famous for his philosophy of education, similarly viewed the moral self as emerging from social related-ness to others: "To learn to be human is to develop through the give-and-take of communication in an effective sense of being an individually distinctive member of a community" (p. 332). For both Mead and Dewey, this socially situated self means that rich moral deliberation is affected not only by the calculation of one's own interests in isolation, but by social interests from which individuals emerge.

Feminist care ethicists (Gilligan, 1982; Noddings, 1984) likewise view moral deliberation as growing out of family relationships. A person making moral decisions, according to care ethics, cultivates her "best self" (Noddings, 1984) from the roots of past strong moral relationships. Unlike moral traditions grounded in intelligence and rationality, care ethics is grounded in exploring our emotional ties to others, which results in a more expansive and diverse moral community. Pragmatist and care ethicists also understand morality as something that can be grown and cultivated; not something that relies on the accident of our birth such as traditional intelligence. If our moral decisions come from our best caring relationships and can be learned, moral commu-nity can be extended to people with intellectual disabilities, not just as moral patients, but as active decision-makers. Because care ethics grew out of a desire to widen the moral community to include the experience of women, it is appro-priate that it could be further expanded to other marginalized communities. Genuinely perceiving the interests and contexts of others is central to care eth-ics. About care ethics and the Ashley Treatment, Kittay (2011, p. 615) wrote:

> because the new parent, if not herself disabled or already the parent of a disabled child, is likely to bring her own ableist biases to the situation, and as the physician is professionally liable to see disability as a medical con-dition only, a fully adequate response will require information from those better situated to provide a perspective from a life lived with disability.

Pragmatist and care ethics, akin to the social model of disability, attempt to understand the interests of individuals in their whole contexts, and see communities, as Kittay suggested, as enriched by diversity.

Similarly, social situatedness can be used to ground relationships with people with declining mental capacities in clinical settings. Hilde Lindemann's (2010) work on caring for adults with dementia includes the idea of using a social narrative structure to help people retain identity. Like Mead, Lindemann conceptualized a self, including moral agency, which emerges from family relationships. Personal identity then results from the shared stories we tell (social narrative). This social self is key to helping people with dementia hold onto their identity and the relationships from which it developed.

Caring about others and empowering their moral agency is integral to pragmatist and care ethics, as well as other ethical movements which ground moral decision making in shared experiences and relationships. They offer a structure to ethical activity that utilizes and promotes rich social experiences in diverse communities. Such ways of thinking about morality, beyond traditions that prioritize rationality, are pluralistic and inclusive and account for how we see real people behaving when we talk about empathy, kindness, generosity, and other values that constitute good relationships.

Moral Engagement Based on Capabilities

The "capabilities" approach outlined by Martha Nussbuam is a good example of how conceptualizing morality in terms of a plurality of capacities and experiences, rather than just rationality, is more inclusive and likely more useful. This approach emphasizes comparative quality of life in terms of individual potential and capabilities and calls on governments to improve quality of life based on this assessment. Nussbaum (2006, 2011) promoted ten capabilities which she believed ought to be supported in every person, regardless of their intellectual capacities. Some capabilities are reminiscent of traditional ethical theories, such as life, bodily health, and bodily integrity, but Nussbaum did not highlight in her list traditional individualistic interests, such as rationality or the right to own property. Although these are not excluded from her list, Nussbaum focused on capabilities that promote quality of life and the potential for human association, such as "senses, imagination, and thought," "emotions," "practical reason," "affiliation," "play," "control over one's environment," and even "being able to live with concern for and in relation to animals, plants, and the world of nature" (2011, pp. 33–34). An important feature of an approach based on capabilities is that it bases morality in activities that can be grown or nurtured. In a letter to Singer, Michael Bérubé (2010, p. 108) wrote "You're looking for things people with Down syndrome can't do, and I'm looking for things they can." Grounding morality in many things that provide us with a good quality of life will allow us to include a greater diversity of capable people in our moral decision making.

A Stronger Moral Community

There are many examples of people who may have ID but who have greater than typical abilities for living according to moral values. Two hallmarks of people with Williams syndrome are limitations in spatial thinking and theory of mind, but they often have a greater desire to connect and share with others than their peers without this condition. Neuroendocrinologist Robert Sapolsky noted that people with Williams have social feelings, such as warmth and empathy, but that on the other hand, "Sociopaths have great theory of mind. But they couldn't care less" (Dobbs, 2007).

Likewise, relationships with people with disabilities often have valuable moral consequences for more typically abled people—in the classroom (Lekan, 2009), in families (Brown, 2009), and in the workplace (Austin & Pisano, 2017). Our moral theories are only as good as their benefits for humanity. Those benefits should go beyond just an individual good will (Kant, 1983/1785). As our moral community becomes more inclusive of people with disabilities, it makes us all better people. As Ian Brown (2009, p. 233) wrote about his son:

> So you can perhaps forgive me for thinking, some days, that Walker has a purpose in our evolutionary project, that he is something more than an unsuccessful attempt at mutation and variation. For thinking, probably vainly, that if his example is noted and copied and "selected," he might be one (very small) step towards the evolution of a more varied and resilient ethical sense in a few members of the human species. The purpose of intellectually disabled people like Walker might be to free us from the stark emptiness of the survival of the fittest.

People with disabilities have much to offer in widening and diversifying the moral community. The "neurodiversity" movement among the autism spectrum community offers a recent model of how inclusion can strengthen both social ties and the workforce. For example, Temple Grandin's unique ability to empathize with nonhuman animals led her to design chute systems for handling cattle at slaughter facilities that are more humane in that they are less likely to cause unnecessary stress and discomfort. Grandin (2017) contended that it is her autism that allows her to imagine the experience of cattle better than a "neurotypical" person would be able to:

> I have learned that there are some people who mainly think in words and I have observed that these verbal thinkers are more likely to deny animals' thought; they are unable to imagine thought without words. Using my visual thinking skills, it is easy for me to imagine myself in an animal's body and see things from their perspective (p. 251).

Similarly, neurodiversity is seen by some employers as offering a competitive advantage. For example, Hewlett Packard and Microsoft are among a growing list of businesses recognizing that people with conditions such as autism or dyslexia often have special skills, like pattern recognition, memory, or mathematics, that make them desired employees. While sometimes companies have to adapt their hiring processes and workplace to accommodate employees who may have special needs, they realize that neurodiversity can be beneficial to business and to the workplace community. A senior vice president at SAP, Silvio Bessa, noted that working to accommodate neurodiverse employees causes him to have greater sensitivity to individuals' needs: "It's made me a better manager, without a doubt" (Austin & Pisano, 2017, p. 98). Other businesses have reported that neurodiversity programs have wider benefits, such as better products, more innovations, greater employee loyalty with lower rates of turnover, and even global corporate citizenship awards (Austin & Pisano, 2017).

The neurodiversity movement may be a good model for inclusive moral communities. If we recognize the positive traits that all humans possess, both individually and in social groups, then marginalized groups might be more valued and more equitably treated. Our conversations might be less about fixing and normalizing people and more about improving quality of life, enhancing supports, and allowing our communities to learn and grow from people with diverse capabilities.

Conclusion

Identifying and labeling ID and associated conditions has a long history among philosophers, psychologists, educators, and medical professionals. In the process, disability became a problem belonging to the person, not a characteristic shared with the surrounding environment. Yet labels may change, even when people do not. A social constructionist view of disability does not deny individual characteristics, but also recognizes the importance of environment and environmental supports in providing opportunities for people with ID.

Accepting that people are social by nature, and that individuals should be social agents in exercising control over their own lives, evokes a new moral community. This approach recognizes the importance of social context and the unique capabilities that may characterize many people with ID. Their rich contributions can make communities more diverse and inclusive, enhancing quality of life, not only for themselves, but also for those around them.

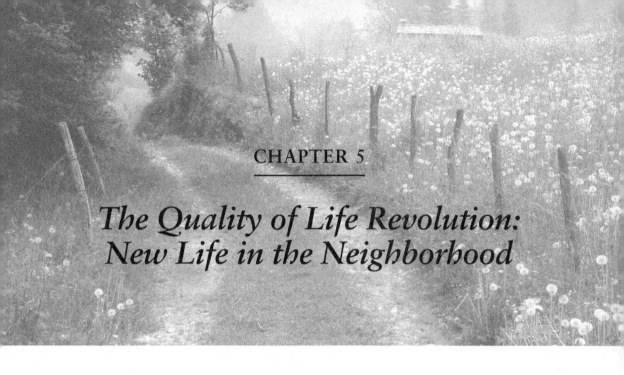

CHAPTER 5

The Quality of Life Revolution: New Life in the Neighborhood

Although recent decades have brought dramatic improvements in the lives of many people with ID, the legacy of the past has too often been marked by denial of rights, limited access to services and supports, and life in sometimes squalid conditions. Those with ID have been subjects of discrimination and victims of abuse, sometimes, as Blatt and Kaplan (1966) so dramatically portrayed, at the hands of those entrusted with their care.

The post-institutional era, however, has brought an emphasis on supportive community services, normalized lives, and the importance of individual and family quality of life. Improved quality of life has been a human aspiration throughout recorded history, and in the past four decades became a focal priority of researchers and others advocating for the well-being of people with ID. In this chapter we review key aspects of the quality-of-life revolution—its meaning, aims, and outcomes. Finally, we discuss the role of the concept of quality of life in relation to the notion of a new moral community.

What We Mean When We Talk about Quality of Life

The Meaning of Quality of Life

People generally aim to live a good life, aspiring to improve their quality of life, not only for themselves, but also for family and friends. Quality of life has been the subject of social science research for many years (e.g., Andrews,

1974; Campbell, 1976; Thorndike, 1939). In recent years, as community services and progressive attitudes have continued to evolve, improvement of quality of life has been a point on which researchers, service providers, advocates, and people with ID themselves could agree. This consensus stands in stark contrast to the views of some early authorities in the field; W. E. Fernald (1902), for example, was convinced that people with ID would find happiness in segregated institutions. After all, he exclaimed, "What more can a boy want!" (p. 489). Nevertheless, given impetus by families, advocacy groups, court decisions, and people with ID themselves, by the late 20th century community-based services saw it as their mission to enhance quality of life. In the 1980s, researchers, too, began to expand the field's understanding of the quality of life of people with ID (e.g., Heal & Chadsey-Rusch, 1985; Keith, Schalock, & Hoffman, 1986; Landesman, 1986), developing measurement tools and exploring the nature and dimensions of quality of life.

In 1995, Cummins reported that more than 100 definitions of quality of life had been published, and the research literature contained reports of more than 1,000 quality-of-life measures (Hughes, et al., 1995). By 2019, a search of the PsychINFO data base returned more than 90,000 entries on the subject of quality of life; clearly, the study and application of the concept of quality of life has expanded greatly. Yet a single clear definition of quality of life has continued to be a difficult target for researchers (Hensel, 2001). Schalock (1996) suggested that a single definition of quality of life, treated as a characteristic belonging to an individual, might not be desirable. An alternative, he observed, would be to think of quality of life as a multidimensional construct, and that researchers would do well to explore those dimensions and their indicators in the lives of individuals.

Other researchers also explored multiple dimensions of quality of life. Hughes and Hwang (1996), examining a number of definitions, concluded that together they encompassed a range of 15 dimensions, among them satisfaction, well-being, community integration, civic responsibility, and personal competence. Felce (1997) described six dimensions: emotional well-being, material well-being, physical well-being, productive well-being, rights (civic well-being), and social well-being; and Keith, Heal, and Schalock (1996), in a seven-country cross-cultural study, found agreement on 10 quality-of-life dimensions: economic security, environment, growth and development, health, individual control, privacy, relationships, rights, satisfaction, and social inclusion. A cross-cultural group of researchers (Schalock et al., 2002) reached consensus on eight dimensions of quality of life: emotional well-being, interpersonal relations, material well-being, personal development, physical well-being, rights, self-determination, and social inclusion. In addition, a consensus has grown that any definition of quality of life should entail not only the work of researchers, but also the views of people with ID and their advocates (e.g., Goode &Hogg, 1994; Keith, 1990; Renwick & Brown, 1996; Ward, 2000). In sum, quality of life has come to connote feelings of well-being, social involvement, the chance to reach individual potential, and the pursuit of excellence in common human values (Schalock et al., 2002)—that is what we mean when we talk about quality of life.

The Scope of Quality of Life

Quality of life exists at the level of the individual (microsystem), the organization or community (mesosystem), and the level of the society or culture (macrosystem; Schalock & Keith, 2016b). Across these levels, a number of foundational core ideas that contribute to quality of life can be identified (Schalock et al., 2002):

1. Individual personal context (life, work, and play settings) is fundamental to quality of life.
2. Different people experience life differently, and people experience life differently at different points in the lifespan.
3. Quality of life is a holistic construct in which different domains interact to constitute the whole.
4. Personal empowerment (making choices, having control) is a major contributor to quality of life.
5. Quality of life requires appreciation of subjective perception—it lies in the eye of the beholder.

These core ideas are embodied in the lives of individuals across at least four important themes that are central to their experience: self-advocacy, community, culture, and aesthetics (Keith & Schalock, 2000).

Self-advocacy implies the work of individuals with ID who are aware of their rights, who take responsibility for their own rights, and who join with others to pursue the interests of the group (Williams & Shoultz, 1982).

Self-advocacy is integrally related to self-determination and empowerment, and these in turn are significant contributors to quality of life (Lachapelle et al., 2005; McDougall, Evans, & Baldwin, 2010; Wehmeyer & Schwartz, 1998). As described in Chapter 4, whether people with ID are able to be self-advocates and empowered to be contributors to moral decisions depends on the conceptualization of moral deliberation and on who is part of the moral community.

Community recognizes that integration into the fabric of one's community is a significant factor in quality of life, and that people whose life experience most nearly approximates that of other members of the community have a higher quality of life. There is also a need to guard against isolation of people with ID in their communities—to recognize the difference between being *present in the community* and truly *living in community* (Chowdhury & Benson, 2011; Keith & Schalock, 2000; Rapley, 2000).

Culture and cultural experience influence individuals' worldviews (Matsumoto & Juang, 2013), perceptions of disability (Watson, Barreira, & Watson, 2000), levels of individuality/communality (Myers, 1992), and intrapersonal/interpersonal sense of self (Markus & Kitayama, 1991). The role of cultural experience in understanding quality of life has been acknowledged by the World Health Organization (Power & Green, 2010), and researchers have noted that, while the core domains of quality of life may be universal, they may be more or less important to individuals across cultures—meaning that assessment of quality of life must be culturally sensitive (Buntinx & Schalock, 2010).

Aesthetics is a theme that recognizes the role of everyday activities—e.g., school, work, relationships, daily decisions—in determining the extent to which people live lives of dignity and grace. Consistent with the views of philosophers John Dewey (1934) and Joseph Kupfer (1983), this perspective seeks to find beauty in the ordinary. Kupfer argued that the beautiful should be a part of everyday life, not only in the obvious places (e.g., art, nature), but in all aspects of how we live and die (including sports and other community-based activities). Some aspects of the aesthetic in individual lives lie in personal stories (Coles, 1989; Taylor & Bogdan, 1996)—a dimension we try to capture in Chapters 7 and 8.

We can say, then, that quality of life is a multidimensional entity, influenced by environmental factors and personal characteristics (Schalock, Keith, Verdugo, & Gomez, 2010). It encompasses a range of human aspirations, including happiness, contentment, success, and satisfaction in the various dimensions of life: emotional, financial, physical, professional, and social (Watson & Keith, 2002). And, in the end, quality of life becomes a part of each person's legacy.

Quality of Life and Families

The focus of much research on quality of life and ID has been, understandably, on the lives of individuals. However, as people with ID are most likely to receive care and support in their family homes, attention has turned to caregivers, who face a number of stressors (e.g., economic, mental health) that can challenge family well-being (Burton-Smith et al., 2009; Cummins, 2001). Families are the primary source of support for children and many adults with ID (Samuel, Rillotta, & Brown, 2012), and support for families, aimed at enhancing their quality of life, is an issue of central importance (Turnbull, Poston, Minnes, & Summers, 2007). As a result, researchers have begun to see family quality of life as an important aspect of policy and practice in the field of ID (Wang & Brown, 2009).

The study of the quality of life of families is based on research on the quality of life of individuals (Wang & Kober, 2011), and, like individual quality of life, family quality of life is multidimensional and inclusive of the individual as well as other family members (Samuel et al., 2012). Among the factors influencing family quality of life, in addition to nature and severity of disability, are available supports, family interactions and relationships, and overall well-being (Bhopti, Brown, & Lentin, 2016). Quality of life is recognized as an important outcome measure to assess the effectiveness of family supports and services (Summers et al., 2005), not only in the U.S., but cross-culturally as well (e.g., Hu, Wang, & Fei, 2012).

Results of a Slovakian study indicated that families of a child with disability experienced a greater need for financial resources than other families, but were equally satisfied with relationships and support from family, friends, and community (Juhásová, 2015). Similarly, Schertz et al. (2016) found that, among Israeli families, quality of life was lowest in the domain of financial well-being, and highest for family relations. And work by Giné et al. (2015)

found higher quality of life in families when a child with ID was over 18 years of age—perhaps suggesting that younger children may result in more family stress. Nevertheless, despite a number of past studies discussing the negative aspects of caring for a child with ID, families have always found means to provide care (Samuel et al., 2012), prompting DeFrain (1999) to suggest that, instead of asking why families fail, we should ask how families succeed.

Quality of Life and a Changing Landscape

Quality of Life in the Hands of People with ID. In an effort to move quality-of-life concepts beyond a simple measure of individual status, researchers have advocated dynamic approaches to enhancement of quality of life by organizations serving people with ID. These approaches include such ideas as appreciation of the unique nature of individual context, the importance of developing new personal opportunities, and the respect inherent in exposure to the dignity of risk (Reinders & Schalock, 2014). Information about quality of life is thus intended to be used—at the individual level to facilitate communication and action to meet individual needs and wishes, at the organizational level to aid programmatic improvement, and at the societal/ cultural level to ensure rights and opportunities (Schalock & Keith, 2016a).

The quality-of-life movement also brought with it a changed perspective on the role of individuals in defining and assessing their own lives. In the past, the quality of life of people with ID was evaluated by others. As the understanding of quality of life has evolved, researchers have recognized the importance of people with ID speaking for themselves, as opposed to relying on the reports of others (Perry & Felce, 2002; Stancliffe, 1995). In addition to reporting their own quality of life, people with ID have also received training to enable them to assist others to report their quality of life (Bonham et al., 2004; Keith & Bonham, 2005; Perry & Felce, 2004). Data collected from people with ID have been used to create public reports of characteristics of service programs (e.g., ARC of Nebraska, 1998, 1999, 2000, 2001, 2002, 2003).

Matters of Life and Death. According to mortality data, people with ID have, on average, a shorter than normal lifespan and reduced life expectancy (Glover et al., 2017). More specifically, people with milder impairment have typical lifespans, and those with more significant impairment typically have shorter lifespans. However, with improved healthcare, the situation is changing, and people are living longer (Forrester-Jones et al., 2017; World Health Organization, 2011). Longer life brings with it an inevitable increase in a variety of conditions associated with aging (e.g., Plichart et al., 2010; Tuffrey-Wijne, 2013), and one additional effect is that people with Down syndrome, whose lifespan increasingly approximates that of the general population, face a greater risk of Alzheimer's disease than do people in the general population (Stancliffe et al., 2012). One response to these demographic changes is recognition that increased attention should be given to end-of-life care for people with ID, and at least one project has attempted to measure quality of life in a specialized end-of-life program (Forrester-Jones et al., 2017). Attention to quality of life of older people is likely to become more common as the life expectancy of people with ID continues to grow and caregivers recognize the importance of quality of life across the lifespan and at the end of life.

Researchers have also begun to explore the need for improved care for children with ID (and their families) with life-limiting or life-threatening conditions. Among children receiving pediatric palliative care, in addition to numerous major medical conditions, nearly half also have a cognitive disability (Feudtner et al., 2011). For children with ID, pain and its management can present particular challenges if care providers assume that pain behavior reflects psychopathology (Breau & Camfield, 2011). Such steps as provision of care coordination, specialized care staff and teams, in-home supports, and respite care can enhance quality of life for both children and families, and may be maximally helpful if integrated early and with the aim of helping children to live as well as possible for as long as possible (Duc, Herbert, & Heussler, 2017). These recent developments in attitudes and supports as people with ID near the end of life hold promise for a new perspective on the value of life and death with ID and the kinds of experiences and memories that lead to a new respect for the legacy of people with ID.

Enhancing Life in the New Moral Community

While people with ID may present special needs for support and staff training, aging need not preclude acceptable levels of physical, psychological, and social well-being. Like other groups, aging people with ID need protection of rights, supports that ameliorate the aging process, and services based on freedom, independence, opportunity, and reduction of the gap between needs and supports (Schalock & Verdugo, 2002). If we can see life as a process, moving through stages toward closure, we can understand the role of death as aesthetically unifying—giving life an entirety, a sense of being whole (Kupfer, 1983). People with ID possess many admirable qualities, among them courage and heroism (Perske, 1980), love (Brown, 2009), initiative (Williams & Shoultz, 1982), and compassion (Kittay, 2010). These are the attributes that make their lives beautiful, contribute to quality of life, help us define new ways of living and dying, and bring new life to the neighborhood.

Psychology and Philosophy: A Powerful Alliance

Blatt (1981) believed that traditional societal perspectives have resulted in a false cultural story about people with ID. However, it follows that changes in the story—that is, changes in the rhetoric defining and describing people with ID—can influence the common understanding of the ID construct (Rapley, 2003, 2004). Philosophers and psychologists have thus undertaken efforts to develop different ways of viewing disability, intelligence, and reason. Psychologists (e.g., Schalock & Keith, 2016a) have recognized the fundamental importance of the domains of interpersonal relationships and personal development to quality of life. Although Western culture has traditionally viewed the self as an individualized, autonomous notion, psychologists now recognize an alternative—an interdependent construal that sees the self in terms of relationships with family, friends, co-workers, and others (Markus & Kitayama, 1991), a perspective less likely to result in social isolation, and in which group membership is of fundamental importance. Similarly, contextual philosophical approaches, such as feminist and pragmatist ethics, stress the importance of a moral perspective aimed toward assisting people to live in emotionally engaged ways (Fesmire, 2003; Noddings, 1984). Thus, psychologists studying quality of life have measured the views of people concerning their social inclusion, community involvement, leisure, and intimacy (Cummins, 1997; Hawkins, 1997; Schalock & Keith, 1993), among other quality-of-life domains.

Study of quality of life necessitates, Taylor and Bogdan (1996) argued, setting aside labels, and, as Keith and Schalock (2016) observed, recognizing that people with ID want to make their world better in the same ways that others do. This means fostering relationships with friends and family, and it entails recognition of the importance of meaningful activities and of love (Helle, 2000). Coupled with an evolving philosophical view that full moral standing should be accorded all those capable of caring (Jaworska, 2010), the quality-of-life movement demonstrates the powerful potential of psychology and philosophy to encourage a new moral community and, with it, the understanding that "The more advanced a civilization becomes, the more it will understand, value, and relate healthily to its members who have severe handicapping conditions" (Perske, 1980).

Vocational Engagement

Unfortunately, the majority of people with ID have difficulty finding a place in the work force (Nord et al., 2013). There are, however, exceptions, such as Collette Divitto. Frustrated that potential employers repeatedly told her she wasn't a "good fit," Divitto decided to prove people wrong. She perfected a recipe and started her own bakery, selling cookies, first in a neighborhood market (Kath, 2016), and then nationally, via her company website (www. colletteys.com/). She has created jobs for other people with disabilities, and she advocates for improved social justice and labor laws—with a focus on ability, rather than disability. She is an example of an individual who has found a new way of living that has improved the quality of her life and the lives of those around her.

It might be natural to hear Collette's story and conclude that new ways of living can be found by people whose disabilities are not severe, and who are not limited by language or attentional deficits, but that others may be unable to tell their stories, or that their interests and aspirations are simply unintelligible or inaccessible. To address this concern, Dennis (2002) examined strategies (e.g., eye contact, emotional comfort, touch, confirming interpretations) and values (e.g., belief the person has something to say, should be respected, and is an equal) that facilitate communication with nonverbal people, as well as some of the impediments (e.g., mistrust, treating person as an object, fear) that make communication difficult. Personal rapport, willingness to share common interests, and reciprocity, Dennis noted, can contribute to communication with people on their own terms, even when others might have assumed them incapable of communication. Such steps can help those with ID at a severe level of impairment to find new ways of living. As described in Chapter 4, there are emerging models in the neurodiversity movement of employers who are willing to adapt hiring practices and workplace environments that enable people with disabilities to become valued employees.

Engagement in Retirement

Difficulties finding employment and historically shorter than average life-spans have been factors that contributed in the past to a general neglect of the notion of retirement for aging people with ID. However, whether they are members of the paid work force or participate in other structured daily activities, they benefit from meaningful activity as they age. Feelings of productivity and positive self-perception contribute to the mental health of aging adults with ID, and researchers have begun to evaluate the role of such meaningful activities as retirement, community service, and volunteerism (Fesko, Hall, Quinlan, & Jockell, 2012), as well as the importance of self-determination and sense of purpose later in life (McDermott & Edwards, 2012). Nevertheless, if aging people with ID are to find a meaningful quality of life in retirement, they will require active support and training (Wilson et al., 2010), as well as acceptance by the community (Bigby, Wilson, Balandin, & Stancliffe, 2011).

End-of-Life Engagement

As the life expectancy of people with ID rises, (Bittles et al., 2002; Patja et al., 2000), they become more likely to outlive their parents and to experience illnesses and other physical conditions commonly associated with aging and end of life (e.g., cancer, cardiovascular disease, dementia; Tuffrey-Wijne, Hogg, & Curfs, 2007; Wiese et al., 2012). Although past research has emphasized bereavement and coping with death, less attention has been focused on the quality of life of people with ID who are approaching the end of life, prompting an interest in the training needs of support staff (Wark, Hussain, & Edwards, 2014) and the possibility that symptoms of physical or mental illness may be overlooked in aging people with ID (Bishop, Robinson, & van Lare, 2013).

As in other areas of quality-of-life research, aging people should be involved as full partners in planning for their own lives (Walsh, Heller, Schupf, & van Schrojensetein Lantman-de Valk, 2001), planning that should take account of the quality-of-life domains (Reilly & Conliffe, 2002). Interestingly, when investigators asked aging people with ID about their desires in life, the themes that emerged were very much like those found in other quality-of-life research; they wanted empowerment, active involvement, safety and security, skills and learning, health and fitness, satisfying relationships, good residential situations, and support (Buys et al., 2008). Although the risk of shrinking social networks is a reality for older people (Bigby & Knox, 2009), there is evidence that individuals with ID can age well, maintaining meaningful, productive lives (Dew, Llewellyn, & Gorman, 2005).

Although most people with ID remain in supported community settings for end-of-life care, some aging people with ID find themselves in nursing homes or other care facilities, due to a variety of medical conditions (Patti, Amble, & Flory, 2010). A disproportionate number of these individuals may enter at relatively young ages and may have difficulty relating to other residents (Pierce, Kilcullen, & Duffy, 2018; Thompson, Ryrie, & Wright, 2004). Because such facilities may focus on health and safety issues, families have expressed concerns about potential social isolation and loss of past relationships (Webber, Bowers, & Bigby, 2014). Research has shown the importance of careful planning for transitions in services and supports, and of the involvement of aging people with ID and their families in decision making (Bigby, Bowers, & Webber, 2011). One proposed model for end-of-life care is a specialized program for older people with ID and multiple needs such as dementia and terminal illnesses. Forrester-Jones et al. (2017) evaluated a program designed to provide palliative and end-of-life care for people with ID, finding good medical quality of life, a high level of individual choice, and good support, although social networks were small.

Whether they live at home or in facilities, people with ID may also benefit from support as they take part in decision making about illnesses and end-of-life care. Specialized nurses and other community support specialists can work with family members to enhance quality of life by ensuring that people with ID understand the aging process, understand major medical concerns, and can voice their desires about medical procedures, including to have or withhold treatment (Tuffrey-Wijne, 2013).

Conclusion

As David Matsumoto (2000, p. xxiii) observed, "Whether African, European, or Asian, gay or straight, living with disabilities or not, the search and striving for a better quality of life is a goal for all of us . . . This striving is the most human of all strivings." With the rise of community services and supports, quality of life became a focal point that brought together people with ID, families, service providers, and researchers, all with the aim of enhancing life experience. Community programs saw it as their role to foster improved quality of life, and researchers took up the challenge to develop new ways to conceptualize and measure it. It became clear that quality of life is individual, personal, and empowering, and that it is as important to people with ID as to anyone else. Contributors to quality of life include advocacy, community, culture, and the aesthetic nature of life experience.

Enhanced quality of life has brought with it an increase in the life expectancy of people with ID, which has brought new attention to the challenges that accompany aging and its associated health-related issues. Thus, while end-of-life discussions historically centered on infants with severe disability, there is increasing need for supports for aging people with ID and end-of-life planning commensurate with a lengthening lifespan. It is important for advocates and support services to facilitate understanding of the aging process and to assist older people to maintain social networks, meaningful activity, and control of their own lives. Perhaps the ultimate legacy of the quality of life movement should be a generation that ages well and, in the end, dies with dignity and grace.

CHAPTER 6

The Supports Movement: Building the New Community

As noted in Chapter 1, Throne (1972) asked why, instead of labeling people as exceptional, we could not instead make the environment exceptional. One way to get beyond the tendency to attribute disability totally to the person is to provide an environment that supports an enhanced level of participation in the activities of one's home and community. Unfortunately, however, people with intellectual disability have often had limited opportunities for participation (Emerson & Hatton, 1996), even though engagement in activity is an important indicator of quality of life (Felce, 2000). This chapter explores the supports paradigm, including its meaning, its relation to our conception of ID, and the role of community and culture in providing supports that may ultimately contribute to the new moral community and the legacy of people with ID.

The Meaning of Supports

Simply put, supports are the resources and strategies essential to foster an individual's growth and development, interests, and well-being (Rapley, 2004). Mostert (2016) identified three aspects of supports: the person's wishes and support needs, everyday provision of the supports, and evaluation of effects of the supports. In other words, supports exist when the environment is responsive to individual needs and desires, and when the results indicate enhanced participation in the affairs of everyday life.

Supports and the Social Construct of ID

In thinking of ID as a construct distinct from prior "defect" conceptions, we can see it as a multidimensional state of functioning reflected in the relation between the person and the environmental context (Wehmeyer et al., 2008). Thus, disability is not a trait that lies inside the person, but instead reflects interaction between the person and the environment (World Health Organization; WHO, 2001). Using the term *human functioning* (WHO, 2001) to encompass an individual's life activities, including body structures and functions, personal activities, and participation, Wehmeyer et al. (2008) showed the role of supports in facilitating congruence between person and environment. A functional definition of disability is consistent with pragmatist philosophy, which views truth as something that happens to an idea, based on context and events (James, 1907/1995), and human behavior as part of a total organism that functions in an environment (Dewey, 1896). Ability or disability, then, are about an interaction between individuals and their contexts, not merely an inherent part of the individuals themselves.

The approach discussed by Wehmeyer et al. (2008) is based on a model developed by the American Association on Intellectual and Developmental Disabilities (Luckasson et al., 2002; Schalock et al., 2010), and further explored by Arnold, Riches, Parmenter, and Stancliffe (2009). Arnold et al. conceptualized supports as an interface between an individual and the environmental context. Thus supports in various forms include people (family, friends, community members, professionals), advocacy, education, technical aids (e.g., adaptive equipment, computerized text readers), funding, and transportation that are intended to improve the connection, or fit, between person and environment. This, in turn, allows for greater community participation. Individual supports planning is a person-centered process, and involves goal setting, resource selection, and strategy development, with the aim of enhancing life quality (Herps et al., 2016).

Assessment of the connection between individuals and their environments does not necessitate deviance-based labeling. As Dewey (1922) claimed, all human activity is interaction between the person and the environment; and Arnold, Riches, and Stancliffe (2011) suggested that assessment of support needs, whether intellectual or physical, could replace traditional diagnostic efforts. Situating disability in the interaction between person and environment not only allows for effective deployment of supports, but may also aid in easing the assumption of incompetence (Dorozenko, Roberts, & Bishop, 2015) and the stigma that has too often been an aspect of the lifelong identity of people with ID (Beart, Hardy, & Buchan, 2005). Reduction of the stereotypes associated with such stigma will result in different, more positive perceptions of people with ID by those in the general population.

Social Supports and Social Commitment

Parents of children and adolescents with ID are vulnerable to high levels of stress (Patton et al., 2016), a circumstance that can result in negative parenting behaviors and resultant adjustment difficulties for the children— consequences that may be mitigated by a number of psychological resources, including social support (Hastings, 2002). Social support is also associated with parental ability to see a crisis as manageable (Hedov, Annerén, & Wikblad, 2002), and emotional support for parents is associated with improved family quality of life (Cohen, Holloway, Dominguez-Pareto, & Kuppermann, 2014). Social support is likewise critical to management of stress for adults with ID who, in the absence of support, may be much more likely to experience mental illness (Scott & Havercamp, 2014); and active support is a good predictor of the quality of life of people with ID having severe impairments (Beadle-Brown et al., 2016).

Peers can provide significant support for students with ID having severe impairments, as Asmus et al. (2017) found in a program using individualized social networks to increase social contacts and friendships with students without disabilities. Social support, including peer support, is also an aid to young adults making the postschool transition to employment (Axel & Beyer, 2013), just as it is to people exercising their rights with the support of committed family members (Hillman et al., 2012). The support needs of the postschool transitional period may be increased by the presence of medical and behavioral challenges, and these needs may spill over into other areas of support, including health and safety, home living, and community living (Seo et al., 2017).

In keeping with the notion that supports should be person-centered, researchers have recognized that support needs change across the lifespan, particularly at the end of life (Moro, Savage, & Gehlert, 2017). Furthermore, it is essential that individuals be involved in developing and evaluating their own support plans (Herps, Buntinx, & Curfs, 2013). To this end, a supportive social environment is associated with resilience in individuals with ID (Hall & Theron, 2016), as are opportunities for independent participation in a variety of activities, including making such personal choices as financial decisions (Stancliff & Lakin, 2007).

As we can see, a wide variety of studies reflect a common theme. Effective support requires social commitment: commitment not only from family members, peers, and staff of schools or social organizations, but also funding agencies and governments. For example, as funding is increasingly distributed on an individual basis, it will be important that resources are not only adequate to provide necessary supports, but also fairly allocated to meet individual needs (e.g., Stancliffe, Arnold, & Riches, 2016). In this way, people with ID may have increased opportunities to fully participate in the activities of their homes and communities, and to be valued as contributing members of their society.

Supports and Community: Ensuring Participation

An essential part of a meaningful life in community is the opportunity and ability to identify personal aspirations, a key aspect of person-centered planning (O'Brien & O'Brien, 2002). It is also essential that the community respect the rights and choices of the individual (Glicksman et al., 2017), and that opportunities for meaningful participation in the activities of daily life are enhanced (Thompson et al., 2009).

Personal Goals and Planning

Following a history in which people were often expected to fit into existing service delivery systems (e.g., Sanderson, 2000) or to simply accept programs or supports without playing an active role in their design (Rose, 2003), services have moved toward more personal, individualized approaches (Dowling, Manthorpe, & Cowley, 2007). Person-centered planning developed with the aim of more centrally involving people with ID, along with family members and other non-paid support people, as partners in individual goal setting and planning (Stineman, Morningstar, Bishop, & Turnbull, 1993). Research has shown that person-centered planning can facilitate greater personal choice, as well as increased contact with friends, family, and the broader community (Holburn et al., 2004; Robertson et al., 2006).

Recent research has suggested that individualized person-centered planning is associated not only with increases in personal outcomes (i.e., achievement of individual goals), but also with increased goal-oriented supports (Gosse, Griffiths, Owen, & Feldman, 2017) and self-determination (Wehmeyer & Bolding, 2001). Among the personal outcomes that can be fostered by the goal setting inherent in person-centered planning is social inclusion, although this effect is dependent on availability of sufficient individualized supports (McConkey & Collins, 2010). Furthermore, in addition to encouraging increased goal setting, person-centered planning may also encourage improved self-esteem and happiness (Wigham et al., 2008). It is important in person-centered planning that individuals be involved in creating their own plans, reflecting their own aspirations, and that plans be evaluated based on accomplishments of the individual person, not the activities of staff (Lawlor, Spitz, York, & Harvey, 2013). Here, as in earlier discussion of supports, we see the importance of putting the needs of the person above the value of a diagnosis (McElvaney, 2011). Finally, we note that participation in one's own planning, as well as provision of needed supports, is an important foundation for respecting and maintaining individual rights (Hillman et al., 2012).

Respect for Rights and Choice

In the United States, a number of federal acts have served to protect the rights of people with ID; noteworthy among these are the *Americans with Disabilities Act* and the *Individuals with Disabilities Education Act* (U. S. Department of Justice, 2009). International recognition of the rights of all people came with the *Universal Declaration of Human Rights* (United Nations, 1948), the *Declaration on the Rights of Mentally Retarded Persons* (1971), and the *Declaration on the Rights of Disabled Persons* (United Nations, 1975). Following many years of work by advocates, these rights were further amplified in the United Nations *Convention on the Rights of Persons with Disabilities* (CRPD; United Nations, 2006). (Interestingly, although the United States signed the Convention, it has never ratified it.) In reviewing the articles of the *Convention*, Verdugo, Navas, Gómez, & Schalock (2012) noted that it advances the cause of rights by virtue of its inclusion of not only individual needs, but also environmental context and supports.

Among the rights identified in the CRPD are the right to live in the community, privacy rights, and the right to participation (Megret, 2008).

Researchers have recognized the importance of systematic monitoring of the rights of people with disabilities (Tichá et al., 2018), and the significant contribution of rights to the quality of life of individuals with ID (Schalock & Keith, 2016c). Supports are integral to enhancement of life (e.g., Schalock et al., 2010), and to the exercise of rights by people with ID (AAIDD, 2015). Thus, if people are to assume their rightful role as participants in the settings of daily life—e.g., home, school, community, relationships, work—they require (and have rights to) the supports that will make such participation possible (Buntinx, 2016).

Opportunity to Participate

Stancliffe et al. (2016) used school transportation as an example of one kind of community support. Although students with disabilities often use expensive segregated transportation, they pointed out, as Haveman et al. (2013) reported, many of those students, with appropriate training, could travel to school independently and less expensively via general public transportation. The segregated service may foster disability, whereas the more independent option would facilitate community engagement, autonomy, and participation. The less expensive choice would also, with enabling community support, be more desirable.

In another example of the value of natural community support, Lee et al. (1997) found that job training provided to workers with ID by inhouse mentors resulted in more social interaction with other workers than did training by an outside job coach. This finding suggests the potential merit of reliance on "natural" community supports in fostering normal social relations and community participation. This point is important in view of research like that of Robertson et al. (2001), who found that many adults living in community residences had very small social networks, particularly beyond paid staff and other people with ID. In conceptualizing the role of supports, Thompson et al. (2009) distinguished between service planning and support planning, with the role of a support plan being to assure participation by identifying resources necessary to bridge the gap between what is (a mismatch between person and living environment) and what could be (experiences and opportunities that the person values). Thus, an individual may receive residential services, yet not meet the goals of community inclusion or development of relationships—a deficit that can be remedied by an appropriate supports plan.

Although many community agencies are typically available to provide services to the general population of older citizens, aging people with ID may not be frequent recipients of these services (Buys & Rushworth, 1997). Accordingly, planning for appropriate supports may be particularly important to these individuals, especially in recognition of the likelihood that their level of social connectedness is lower than that of other older community residents (McCausland, McCallion, Cleary, & McCarron, 2016). Research has shown that aging people with ID (and their caregivers) desire supports that will allow them to maintain and enhance their social networks, and to age in place (Shaw, Cartwright, & Craig, 2011). Like school children and working adults, aging people with ID simply want the kind of support that enables normal opportunities for participation in their communities and the dignity and respect that come with such participation.

Culture and Support

The availability of resources, including supports, varies widely across cultures. Similarly, cultures have differing views of disability, health, happiness, understanding of the self, and other constructs that contribute to perceptions of people with ID and their quality of life. Nevertheless, support needs and the desire of people to play meaningful roles in their communities are universal.

Cultural Understanding

The degree of social inclusiveness experienced by people with disability in a culture plays a key role in determining whether the culture supports healthy communities, more or less disability stigma, and opportunities for greater participation (Mpofu et al., 2018). Researchers have long known that attitudes toward inclusion and participation of people with ID vary across cultural groups (e.g., Thomas, 1957); for example, Sheridan and Scior (2013) found that young British South Asians were less likely than White British people to support social inclusion of people with ID. In a California study of maternal attitudes, Blacher, Begum, Marcoulides, & Baker (2013) found that Latino mothers reported higher positive effects of the presence of a child with ID than did Anglo mothers. The notion of disability too often conveys culture-based negative social meanings (Lawson, 2001), although the World Health Organization International Classification of Functioning (2009) asserted that disability is a universal human experience.

In a discussion of disability concepts that are likely to be misunderstood in the absence of cultural context, Mpofu et al. (2018) identified the following:

- Universality of disability experience. Approximately 15 percent of the world's population have a disability, and the large majority of disabilities are not visible.
- Disability identities. People are more likely to self-identify with disability in cultures that do not marginalize or exclude those with disabilities.
- Culturally diverse perspectives of disability. In addition to cultural views about community participation or autonomy, cultures vary in the extent to which attitudes toward disability are entwined with religion, beliefs about medical practices, and cultural myths and traditions.

Furthermore, attitudes vary, not only across specific cultures and between ethnic minority groups within cultures (Scior, Addai-Davis, Kenyon, & Sheridan, 2013), but also along such dimensions as horizontal and vertical collectivism and individualism (e.g., Ditchman et al., 2017). And some cultures have no language to label or describe disability (Mpofu et al., 2018), thinking of the individual not as one who stands apart as different, but simply as one of the group—and what is good for the life of the group is good for the individual (Pengra, 2000). Clearly, views of people with ID and their needs are understood differently by different cultural groups.

Supports and Cultural Values

Researchers have studied cultural views of desirable goals and practices that exist within different societies. Ideas about what members of a culture collectively consider right and good are known as values (Matsumoto & Juang, 2013). Values may influence how people with ID are viewed within a culture, and they may color the kinds of supports that individuals need or receive. The most widely known approach to analyzing cultural values is the set of dimensions described by Hofstede (2001). These dimensions include individualism-collectivism, power distance, masculinity-femininity, uncertainty avoidance, and long-term orientation. Of these, individualism-collectivism is the most frequently researched, and perhaps of most interest in the context of supports for people with ID.

Individualism-collectivism is a cultural dimension reflecting the extent to which the interests of the individual or the group prevail in a cultural setting (Keith, 2012). Provision of supports in a strongly person-centered program might be seen as reflective of an individualistic perspective in, for example, residential settings committed to supporting individual choice and life as nearly as possible in the way each person wants it (e.g., Bigby & Beadle-Brown, 2016). On the other hand, a more collectivistic perspective emphasizes the well-being of the group, as suggested by the Lakota view that "What's good for the people would be good for him [a person with ID], because he is part of the community" (Pengra, 2000, p. 193). In collectivist cultures the support of families or clans (as opposed to individual effort or responsibility) is important to caregivers for people with ID, although that support can be offset by the loss of face and stress caused by cultural stigma (Chiu et al., 2013). It seems likely that strong supports embody the best of both individualistic and collectivistic perspectives, respecting and advocating for individual rights and goals, while also fostering group participation and the welfare of individuals as members of a community of people. In this sense, an overriding cultural value characterizing good supports may be strong positive regard for people with ID and the perception (by those providing supports) that they are individuals "like us" (Bigby, Knox, Beadle-Brown, & Clement, 2015).

In any event, whatever the cultural backdrop, the lives of people with ID, like those of all people, are played out at the individual level. Thus, if we take seriously the aim of full group or community participation, and the value of every citizen, it is necessary for that broader cultural vision to be experienced at the level of each person with ID.

Individualizing a Cultural Vision

Although cultural dimensions such as individualism-collectivism have proven useful in the study of societies around the world, each life is lived at the level of the individual. And at that level, assumptions about cultural values can frequently be mistaken. There are many collectivists living in individualistic countries, and many individualists can be found in collectivistic countries (Matsumoto & Juang, 2013). Thus, at the individual level, people may view themselves in differing ways. In particular, researchers have noted that some people define themselves in terms of their relationships with others—parents, siblings, fellow students, coworkers, and friends—while some find their sense of self in an independent view, autonomous and distinct from others (Markus & Kitayama, 1991). This distinction may be significant in planning supports for people; for instance, although it may be tempting to assume that social immersion is an aim to which everyone could (or should) aspire (an interdependent self-perception), some individuals may in fact prefer to see themselves as autonomous, and perhaps prefer more solitary activities (an independent self-perception). The key point is that those providing supports should be sensitive to the wishes of the person with ID.

Culture becomes individual in other ways as well. Cultures vary widely in such characteristics as government, healthcare, urbanization, geographic topography, human service systems, transportation, religion, education, and more. As Stancliffe et al. (2016) observed, for example, the transportation needs (and associated training) of an individual living in a rural area may be quite different from those of a city dweller. Those living in mountainous rural areas may be isolated from services. Likewise, recreational opportunities or availability of healthcare in particular communities will influence the supports required by individuals wishing to access them. In the realm of healthcare, for example, people in Western cultures are likely to receive contemporary biomedical care, but those living in other places (e.g., Hindu countries such as India) may also receive treatment from traditional healers (Gurung, 2011). Although we often think of culture on a national or international scale, for each citizen, each person with ID, culture and the supports it can provide are, in the end, an individual matter.

Conclusion

If we consider ID not merely as an immutable characteristic of the person, but instead as an indicator of a mismatch, or gap, between person and environment, it then follows that an environmental context capable of bridging the gap will improve life for the individual. It is the aim of the supports paradigm to bridge, or at least narrow, the gap. Supports may include physical aspects of the environment, in the form of such items as wheelchairs, computerized devices, or adaptations in architecture or signage; or they may include personal support from individuals who provide training, or assistance with personal or household tasks.

Supports represent a commitment: a social commitment to sustain the assistance needed by the individual and a commitment to a needs assessment and planning process that is centered on the person and the person's goals and desires. Commitment to person-centered planning and supports also represents a commitment to the rights of the person, including the right to make individual choices. The aim is to enhance personal participation in the community in ways that are culturally normative and consistent with individual aspirations, to see people with ID ". . . in the mainstream of life, living in ordinary houses in ordinary streets, with the same range of choices as any citizen . . ." (King's Fund Centre, 1980). Meaningful support leads to more meaningful lives and more satisfying legacies.

CHAPTER 7

Exemplary Cases: Lives Well Lived

Increasingly, people with ID achieve recognition for what they can do rather than what they cannot (Bérubé, 2010), and some of their achievements are truly extraordinary. And, like any other family members, they experience joy, suffer tragedy, laugh, cry, and make memories.

This chapter discusses some of the ways in which people with ID are making noteworthy contributions by virtue of their skills, training, and determination, as well as the supports that have assisted them in their achievements. This chapter also includes stories of others who are quietly creating their own legacies, out of the limelight, but in the warm glow of family and friends. In the process, these people have lived a life of dignity, with the respect of those around them.

Call Me by My Name: Dignity and Respect

Wolfensberger (1988) argued that people with ID commonly possess prosocial characteristics, or "gifts" (e.g., joy, trust, spontaneity) that are too often overlooked, especially by those whose perceptions are based on a deficit orientation. Wolfensberger (1983, 2011) further declared that the way we value people depends on how we perceive their social roles and relationships, and that it should be our aim to create, support, and defend valued social roles for people with ID. This is important, Wolfensberger (2000) asserted, because social roles give a person a place in society and define the person's relationships with others. Wolfensberger (2011) called this idea *social role valorization*, from the meaning of valor as *value* or *worth*. How people are perceived in the web of social relationships is instrumental in how much we value (or devalue) them, and this in turn helps to determine what other social goods people are afforded. For example, if we see people with ID as coworkers, companions, neighbors, political participants, taxpayers, and otherwise active members of communities, it is more likely that we will value them more and see that they have access to supports, companionship, and other social goods that all humans need. Viewing people in this way also moves us in the direction of true justice and morality (Wolfensberger, 2000).

Ordinary People, Extraordinary Character

Increasingly, modern cultures recognize the value, the *valor*, of people with ID and the roles they play in society. As described in Chapter 5, Collette Divitto, a woman with ID, established a bakery and succeeded in expanding it to market her cookies nationally (Sholl, 2016). After being rejected by several potential employers, and with the support of a neighborhood market, she transformed her skills into a socially valued role, created her own business, and in the process created jobs for others as well.

Ollie Webb

Another persistent woman, Ollie Webb, was born in the Great Depression and survived many years of life in a large institution for people with ID before moving to a community placement when she was in her 40s. There, she was discovered by community worker Tom Miller, who found her living in the basement of a bad nursing home where her freedom was limited and she was engaged in poorly supervised work tasks. Tom helped to put in place supports that allowed Ollie to move to an apartment with congenial housemates and a supportive staff member who provided assistance with such tasks as shopping and cooking (Webb, 2002). Ollie became an active participant in her community, where she learned to sew, cook, use public transportation, and engage in a variety of community events.

Ollie married, divorced after a few years, then took in and supported others, teaching them cooking and other skills of daily living. For 17 years, Ollie held a job where she prepared sandwiches, soup, and salads, and carried out a variety of other food preparation tasks. Ollie became a property owner and was a leader in advocating for rights and opportunities for people with ID. Despite being forced to retire after a heart attack, Ollie continued to lead a satisfying life, including a good relationship with her daughter, who had also been a resident of a large state institution for a time.

As an advocate, Ollie received support from Tom and others, serving as president of a self-advocacy group and establishing herself as a powerful voice for those she called "my people." In discussing her advocacy work, Ollie said "I find out what the people want, and I try to help them get it. I try to teach them to help themselves. I also do public speaking. I go to conferences and conventions and speak to the public . . ." (Williams & Shoultz, 1982, p. 41). Ollie was proud of her ability to speak out on behalf of those who could not speak for themselves. Her leadership enabled her to speak not only at statewide conventions, but at other gatherings across the U.S. and in England (Webb, 2002).

In 1998, in her home city of Omaha, Ollie's legacy was recognized by dedication of the Ollie Webb Center, a community resource providing a range of advocacy, training, and support services. Ultimately, this extraordinary person wanted to be remembered as someone who would speak for those who needed a voice, and as an ordinary person: "I am the same as you. I got a name, and I want you all to call me by my name" (Webb, 2002, p. 57).

Yet many people with ID live quiet lives in ordinary communities, going to work or school, and spending time with family and friends. As Perske (1980, p. 73) noted in discussing integration of people with ID in communities,

> It started as a very big deal, but as the changes take place, most people will see them as no big deal at all. Acceptance of people with developmental disabilities will be so commonplace that we will only wonder why it took so long to come about.

Randy Bell

Randy is a 27-year-old man who was adopted as a child into a family that includes three older siblings and two younger ones. He has lived all his life in his home community, and now enjoys supports from a local agency, including residential support in an extended family home consisting of Randy and a young adult roommate who receives funding from the agency. Randy loves life in his apartment with his roommate, a congenial companion who drives him to work, and with whom he plays guitar and keyboard music. They are also sometimes joined by a couple of other musician friends.

For five years, and with agency support, Randy has worked as an office assistant, a job that includes filing, laminating documents, document shredding, and other office tasks. He feels a sense of community, both at work and at home, and says the support he receives from the agency "has made me a better person." After being home schooled as a young child, Randy had a combination of home schooling and public school during his high school years. He has also taken courses at a local community college and reports that his favorite class was U.S. History. Randy has traveled to Washington, DC, where he especially appreciated the opportunity to visit historical sites that he had read about. When he watches television, he particularly likes documentaries.

Randy's parents live nearby, and he and his brothers and sisters gather frequently at his parents' home for family meals. He also keeps in touch with a number of friends in the community. Despite having what he calls "low vision," Randy likes to cook for himself and his roommate, and says that he likes to experiment with cooking. His self-deprecating sense of humor is evident when he talks about his kitchen skills: "I'm a good microwaver!" Randy's sense of humor is also apparent in his appreciation of jokes and riddles, and in his acknowledgement that "Most of my jokes are stinkers."

In discussing how he would like to be remembered, Randy says he is an animal lover (with a feisty cat that he loves), a musician who loves to get together and play with his friends, and a reliable friend to anyone who needs to talk with someone. Perhaps most important, he says, is that he cares deeply about people; he worries about where the world is going, but believes that everyone has the capacity for good. To that end, he says, "I try my best one day at a time."

Walker Brown

Walker Brown was born with cardiofaciocutaneous syndrome, a rare congenital condition producing multiple physical disorders, as well as ID (e.g., Niihori et al., 2006). Walker has required significant support in personal care, mobility, and communication throughout his life (Miki, 2017), and by the time he was three years of age his medical record was 10 pages long (Brown, 2009). Walker communicates via grunts or nudges, and at age 14, according to his father, looked about 10 and had cognitive skills typical of a child of 2 or 3 (Brown, 2011).

Walker's father has said that the tube feeding, diaper changing, and other tasks associated with Walker's care are the easy part. More important, he wrote, were questions about Walker's inner life—whether his life had meaning or purpose that he was unable to express. Eventually, it became clear that the answer was yes, that Walker responded gleefully when he was included in conversation, that he was happy when his sister read to him, or when he successfully cleared a table of anything resting on it—whether papers, glasses, or smart phones (Brown, 2011). In that moment, succeeding in tricking his watchful parent, and exerting control in his own way, Walker became an equal in a situation that he had created on his own terms.

In the same way, encounters with people with severe disability, when both parties may be uncertain how to interact, can make both participants equals—a situation enabling (and in fact requiring) a new way to connect (Miki, 2017). After all, Walker's father says, "The frame of any human relationship exists behind a veil of words, and sometimes sounds like something other than it is. . . Walker and I don't compound our confusion with words. We prefer noises" (Brown, 2009, p. 246). Eventually, it became possible to see beyond the demands of day-to-day care, and to find the value in a life that a geneticist once called "a deleterious effect of nature" (Brown, 2011). In the meantime, Walker learned to help his wheelchair-bound classmates, collecting and putting away their backpacks when school begins, and returning them at the end of the day (Miki, 2017). Walker may never be recognized for his achievements in the eyes of the world, but he is an integral part of his family, and he has taught those around him many good lessons. Perhaps, as his father says, "The more we move away from our focus on being the best, and instead work on how we are relating to other people—that seems more important to me these days" (Miki, 2017, para. 8).

Lisa Fennell

At the age of 39, Lisa has worked for eight years in the dietary department of a nursing care facility. She cooks, washes dishes, delivers food carts, and engages in a variety of other tasks required by her department. She is efficient in her work, and well-experienced, having done similar jobs in other facilities for about 20 years. Her role at work, she says, is important to the people she serves, and they miss her when she is not there. She likes her boss, who is helpful, supportive, and communicates well with her. Her boss does not treat her as if she has a disability, but is very understanding and helpful if "I give her the confused look or I don't get it." Lisa gets along well with the residents of the nursing facility, at least in part because she understands their needs and helps to meet those needs.

Lisa has two brothers and a sister, and lives in a pleasant neighborhood in a house with her sister and brother-in-law. An additional housemate is a 17-year-old young man, a family member with autism, and Lisa provides him with support and help with household tasks. She has taught him to ride the bus, for example, and goes on outings with him. She enjoys this role, and she enjoys independence in her home and work life. She uses both buses and taxis for work and other community activities, and sometimes receives rides from her father, who lives nearby. Although she has tried to learn to drive, she has concluded that this may not be something she wants to do. Lisa is proud of the fact that her older brother and her sister are college graduates.

One of Lisa's brothers works and lives in Russia, and she has visited there, seeing both St. Petersburg and Moscow. She has also traveled to Ireland, Germany, and Italy with a church group. Lisa has been to Washington, DC several times with her sister, and has enjoyed visiting Florida, California, Hawaii, and Boston. She is proud of the fact that she adapts well to new experiences and can navigate in unfamiliar places by identifying landmarks that she can "mark in my head." She also loves living with her sister, with whom she has resided for a long time. "You know," she says, "it's kind of like a marriage. In a marriage you have a honeymoon phase, then no honeymoon phase and you just end up getting along just peachy. Well, we get along just peachy."

Although Lisa communicates well using spoken language, she says she has difficulty communicating in writing, that she is not a good speller, and that she is not good at math and time concepts. However, with the help of her sister, she has learned to use technological supports to allow her to access such communication aids as voice recognition text messages. She is a frequent user of telephone and text messaging to keep in touch with friends and family. One of her brothers, Lisa says, also has ID, and they communicate well with each other. Lisa also speaks knowledgeably about her ID and her experiences as a student in special education classes, saying that she had good experiences in school and learned such practical skills as using the bus system. She has also had occasion to employ her first-aid skills, providing care for an injured family member with a serious cut until emergency personnel arrived.

Lisa is active in her community, engaging in a variety of community organizations and activities. She has taken cooking classes and has participated in Special Olympics. She values community events organized for adults with ID, including bowling, movies, and restaurant meals. Although she does not keep in touch with people from her school, Lisa enjoys the company of people with whom she has worked, and they participate together in various activities in the community, and occasionally go together to a shopping mall. She sometimes takes a bus to these gatherings, and at other times rides with friends who drive. She also enjoys time with her two dogs, calling them her babies and her best friends, and is pleased that they sleep with her.

Lisa has had experience with death in her family, including the deaths and funerals of an uncle and her mother. She also worries about an aunt who is the only remaining member of her own immediate family. When discussing funerals, Lisa says "Mine better be a party," meaning, she says, a celebration. Lisa would like people to remember her as a happy, kind person who has only two fears in life: a fear of escalators and of snorkeling. "I'm deathly afraid of escalators. When I go to the mall, I don't take the escalator; I take the elevator 10 times over." As for snorkeling, Lisa is determined to overcome her fear: "I'm going to Hawaii soon and I'm going to snorkel. I'm not going to let my fear of snorkeling overcome me."

Among Lisa's satisfactions are the facts that she has lived to see a minority person (Barack Obama) elected President of the U.S., that laws have changed to allow gay people to marry, and that people with disabilities and Native American people have rights that make discrimination less likely than in the past. She has strong political views and votes, she says, for laws to make things better, and she pays her taxes and her bills. In her view, "I have to support myself like everybody else, no matter if I have a disability or not." Lisa's legacy will be that she was a kind person, a valued family member, and a solid, responsible citizen—social role valorization at work.

Noelia Garelia

When she was a young child, a nursery school teacher rejected Noelia Garella due to her Down syndrome, calling her a "monster" (The Logical Indian, 2016). However, since 2012 Noelia has worked in public education, becoming a nursery school teacher herself in Cordoba, Argentina (Independent, 2016). Despite being declared unfit by one training program, Noelia completed a teaching course, earned a teaching certificate, and became an assistant before receiving a promotion to teacher in 2016 (Schreiber, 2016).

With the support of her parents and instructors, Noelia overcame the doubts of others that a person with ID could work in a school, and with the support of her parents and instructors, Noelia was able to achieve her dream. As the doubters came to know her, they too became advocates for the decision to hire Noelia as a teacher. Her students, however, did not have to overcome doubts or prejudice; they simply love it when she reads to them and tells them stories (Schreiber, 2016). At the age of 31, many years after facing rejection by those who once saw her as a misfit (Kraft, 2016), Noelia became a valued member of the school staff.

The concern of people at Noelia's school was whether someone with ID would have the capacity to be in charge of a class (Independent, 2016). Yet soon her students, two- and three-year-olds, were gathered around her with affection and rapt attention. A former administrator at her school observed that "She gave what the children in the nursery classes most appreciate, which is love" (Kraft, 2016). That sentiment reflects Noelia's aim, expressed in her own words when she says "I adore this. Ever since I was little, I have always wanted to be a teacher, because I like children so much" (Independent, 2016). Noelia's legacy will not be the stigma too often associated with ID; instead, she will be remembered as a loving teacher who, against all the odds, found a valued place in the life of her community.

Conclusion

Despite policies and laws intended to ensure respect and social inclusion, many people still face misunderstanding and negative attitudes (Seewoorut-tun & Scior, 2014). Yet people with ID, like any other people, occupy important places in their families and communities. They live satisfying lives, enjoy significant relationships, and hold valued jobs. In return, they deserve respect and recognition, not as faceless members of a stigmatized group, but as equal partners in their society. They simply want to be recognized as ordinary individuals and to be known, as Ollie Webb said, "by my name."

People with ID across cultures are making their voices heard and gaining the attention and respect of their fellow citizens. In addition to the U.S., these leaders are speaking out in a number of countries including: Australia, China, Germany, India, and Uruguay (Keith & Schalock, 2016); Belgium (Van Hove & Schelfhout, 2000); Canada (Ryan & Griffiths, 2015); Finland (Helle, 2000); Israel (Goldman, 2000); and the United Kingdom (Williams & Shoultz, 1982). These are people asking only for equal treatment, people who want to be remembered for their kindness and decency. As Ian Brown (2009, p. 284) noted, in quoting geneticist Bruce Blumberg, it is ". . . a mistake to think of them as lesser than. There's no lesser than. There's just different from. It isn't just great minds that matter. It's great spirits too."

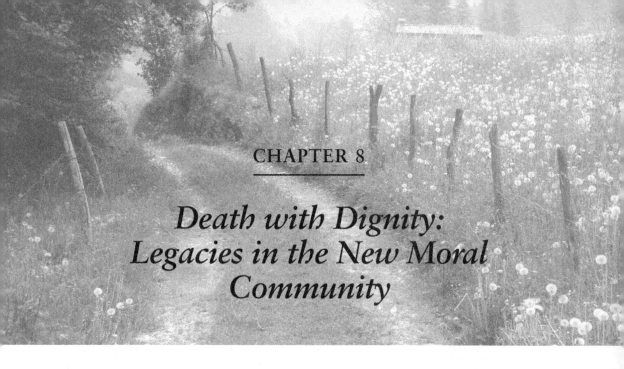

CHAPTER 8

Death with Dignity: Legacies in the New Moral Community

In Chapter 3 we discussed some of the shameful ways that people with ID have died in anonymity and isolation, sometimes lost to memory. Our history as a culture is replete with stories of neglect, denial, and abuse—a history that prompted President John F. Kennedy, speaking in the 1960s of the state of affairs for people with ID in the U.S., to describe the U.S. as a developing country, and that led leaders in the field to ask *What went wrong?* (Dybwad, 1999). One of the things that went wrong, Wolfensberger (e.g., 2011) argued, was a cultural failure to value and accept others—a failure remedied, Blatt (1999c) believed, only by those who can get beyond labels and see everyone as a part of humanity.

In this chapter we discuss the meaning of life and death in the new moral community. What are the implications of thinking differently about people with ID and how might our perceptions alter the opportunity for people to live with respect and die with dignity? We can look to the memory of those whose lives stand as examples of decency, leadership, humor, and heroism—of humanity at its best.

Reflecting on Life and Legacy

In a new moral community, disability lies in the discrepancy between individual needs and environmental supports. It is a community where we all meet each other halfway, where we help and trust each other (Webb, 2002). Everyone is respected as a fellow human, a fellow citizen, and we all complement one another; where one is weak, another is strong. We seek a community in which people do not live and die in isolation, but instead actually *know* one another (Perske, 1980) and live not just in the community, but *in community* (Rapley, 2000).

In a true community we can seek supports to enhance the opportunities available to people with ID, to improve upon a situation in which a majority of adults with ID are unemployed or under-employed (U.S. Equal Opportunity Commission, 2011) and only 16 percent of children with ID spend most of their school day in general classes (McFarland et al., 2018). Resources are required to support people in a life of dignity and respect, although it is essential to note the importance of appropriate individualized supports (i.e., it is an over-simplification to think that more support is always better; Stancliffe, Arnold, & Riches, 2016). Thus, current social conditions can be changed, and people's lives can be improved, but we must be prepared to provide the resources necessary to support such change, and to ensure that supports reflect the dignity that people with ID deserve (e.g., Reid, Rosswurm, & Rotholtz, 2018).

Just as people with ID desire a life of dignity and respect, so should they be assured dignity in death. In a statement on caring at the end of life, the American Association on Intellectual and Developmental Disabilities (2012a) set forth four key principles: dignity, respect for autonomy, life, and equality. These principles are meant to make clear that all people, with or without disability, are equally valuable; that, as much as possible, the desires of people with ID should be honored; that caregivers (not just medical professionals) should promote and protect their rights in making end-of-life decisions; and care at the end of life should be equally available to all, without regard to disability. In other words, people with ID should receive the same respect, the same treatment options, and the same dignity in death as anyone else. These aims have sometimes been complicated by both substandard treatment and inflexibility of laws in some states, resulting in a more difficult death for people with ID (Lahey, 2018).

One approach to ensuring dignity at the end of life is the treatment framework known as *dignity-conserving care* (e.g., Chochinov, 2002), which has been adopted for use with people with ID (Lutfiyya & Schwartz, 2010). As

Chochinov reported, the approach incorporates eight important dignity-conserving perspectives:

1. Continuity of self—Intact sense of self despite illness.
2. Role preservation—Ability to retain usual roles to maintain congruence with prior self-view.
3. Maintenance of pride—Maintaining a positive sense of self-respect.
4. Hopefulness—Seeing a sustained purpose or meaning in life.
5. Autonomy/control—Ability to maintain a feeling of control over life circumstances.
6. Generativity/legacy—Taking comfort in knowing that something of one's life will transcend death.
7. Acceptance—Ability to accommodate changing life circumstances.
8. Resilience/fighting spirit—Determination to overcome illness or to maximize quality of life.

Although dignity may be understood and experienced differently by different people, the notion that people with ID should receive the same kind of treatment as other people, and that they make enduring contributions to the lives of others, should be central to an understanding of their lives and legacies. It may sometimes be difficult for others to know what the person with ID wants at the end of life, but respect for the autonomy of the individual seems important in at least three key contexts: when new information is available about the person's diagnosis, prognosis, or treatment; when care needs and personal wishes change near the end of life; and when important treatment decisions must be made (Bekkema, de Veer, Hertogh, & Francke, 2014). One way to facilitate dignity and personal involvement at the end of life is to be certain that individuals' preferences and values are understood and well documented earlier in life, thus improving the chances that their wishes will not be overlooked in end-of-life decision making (Stein & Kerwin, 2010). A dignified death may well depend upon the opportunity to experience a dignified life. In the next section we relate the stories of exemplary people who lived well, died with dignity, and left behind compelling legacies.

What's Past Is Prologue

As people with ID live increasingly longer, it is important that they understand illness, end-of-life decisions, dying, and death (Surrey and Borders

Partnership, 2012). And it is the lives they lead that create the legacies by which they are remembered by those who survive them. Here we present the stories of four memorable people. Each of them lived a full life, a life experienced *in community*, and although they were very different people, they have in common that they are missed, and that they contributed in substantial, meaningful ways to the lives of those around them. Their lives were prologue to an enduring legacy.

Mark Powell

When Mark was born, the doctor's diagnosis was Down syndrome, with ID at a severe level of impairment. Mark's parents were advised to place him in an institution. At the institution at which he resided, there was little expectation that Mark could accomplish anything. In the absence of significant treatment and in the presence of joint pain and swelling related to juvenile rheumatoid arthritis (JRA), he stopped walking and sat on the floor, where he discovered that, if he "played it cute," other people would do nearly anything for him. As a result, he developed a positive, engaging personality and self-taught speech. He could charm and manipulate anyone.

Eventually, at a time when there was a movement to reduce the census of the institution, Mark moved to a foster home. There, while spending his days in a community developmental center, he met the parents who would adopt him and make him a part of their family. As it turned out, Mark's development was not slowed by Down syndrome; his biggest challenges were kyphoscoliosis (a combination of outward and lateral curvature of the spine), JRA, short stature (about three feet in height), and the loss of much of his hair due to physical stress. He also wore orthopedic shoes, often with leg braces. The adaptations necessitated by these various physical challenges provided few barriers for Mark. He attacked school and life with enthusiasm. He was, at least in his own mind, a great dancer, and he loved school dances. He realized he didn't have John Travolta moves . . . but he had moves, with the necessary adaptations.

When Mark reached high school, his first mathematics class was exciting. He would learn the basics: addition, subtraction, multiplication, and division. On the first day of class he arrived at home after school with homework—complex homework. It would take all night . . . but he was determined to do it. Then, at age 15, the big topic in Mark's home was the exciting question of when he would drive—and his younger brother was just as excited. Together, as they had done so many times before, they were creative, engaging in problem solving, working out logistics, identifying the necessary adaptations. With a driver's license, Mark dreamed, going out on an unsupervised date would be awesome! Perhaps, Mark's father says, there were times when he and Mark's mother pushed too hard, but more often, he says, they underestimated Mark's capability.

Unfortunately, Mark's health challenges became more serious and his body weak. A three-page doctor's letter laid out the diagnosis and the options. The prognosis was not good. Option one: do nothing and expect death within a couple of years due to physical breakdown. Option two: two massive seven-hour surgeries, each carrying some probability of death. As a result of many visits over more than a decade, the doctor had become a friend who highly respected Mark. The letter was terrifying, not easy reading for Mark's parents, and they discussed how best to present its contents to their son. They wanted him to be a part of the decision, or perhaps to make it himself . . . but he was 15. Yes, he had been at the doctor's visits, listening to the scientific explanations and discussion of negative findings, directed to his parents. But when it was time to discuss the issue, Mark's parents wanted to thoroughly explain the letter, taking as long as it needed. To their surprise, when the meeting started, Mark interrupted, saying he had already read the letter, having found it on the coffee table. Further, he wanted to proceed with the surgeries. He knew it was risky, but the other choice, doing nothing and dying in a year or so, was just not an option. Yes, his father says, they were pushy parents, but once again, Mark exceeded their expectations.

Mark chose surgery and, sadly, died in the hospital. A memorial gathering, attended by a large crowd of family, friends, and neighbors, was a true celebration of his life, with memories, laughter, poetry, and the exceptional sense of community that exists in the presence of genuine love and friendship. Later, at Mark's home, the celebration continued with his favorite meal: pizza and chocolate cake. There was talk of his sly sense of humor, his boundless determination, and his big smile. This small boy with a big heart always opted for life, and in his way imparted a kind of wisdom that is long remembered and a legacy embodying the kind of dignity and respect to which we all might aspire.

Tom Houlihan

Tom Houlihan was a gregarious man with great self-confidence. Although he worked for many years in a community thrift store, Tom was supported by family and friends, and never received organized agency services. Prior to his longstanding job at the store, Tom worked for a time at a car wash. Tom's brother was a major source of support, and Tom, in turn, helped to look after his mother late in her life. Effusive and outgoing, Tom was an active participant in his church and in the Knights of Columbus. Speaking of his early life, Tom said "I lived with my parents in the community when I was growing up. At one time they were talking about putting me in an institution when I was little, but the family said no" (Williams & Shoultz, 1982, p. 42).

Tom was a friend to nearly everyone he met, and frequently invited people to his home. He was best man at the wedding of his friends Tom and Janet, and frequently visited and phoned them. He became involved in advocacy groups in his community, and though he was nervous at first, he became an eloquent spokesman for people with ID. In speaking of his first appearance at a public hearing, Tom said "Of course, I was really nervous that night. My left hand was shaky in holding that microphone, and then all of a sudden my left leg started to shake. I mentioned all my friends over the microphone that night. I also did a lot of public speaking when I went to England for the Campaign for Mentally Handicapped People" (Williams & Shoultz, 1982, p. 42). Tom went on to become a fearless advocate, often recommending that groups speaking out for their own rights should invite such authority figures as the state governor to attend their meetings.

Like many people with Down syndrome (e.g., Harley et al., 2015), Tom developed Alzheimer's disease, and died in his early fifties. His friends say that Tom, like many aging people with ID, would have benefitted from better community supports, including retirement services. Tom was widely known in his community, and is well remembered as a thoughtful, friendly man who was an advocate for his fellow citizens.

Eric Ebacher

Eric died suddenly at the age of 34, possibly as a result of a pulmonary embolism. Born with hydrocephalus, Eric underwent 30 surgeries by the age of two and had, his brother says, an uphill battle. Although Eric did not learn to tie his own shoes until he was in his twenties, he eventually became able to learn nearly anything by seeing and then doing it. Although he could understand abstract concepts, Eric needed to *see* in order to learn to *do*.

Following deterioration of his home situation, Eric arrived at his brother's door. His brother took him in, and there he learned the skills of independent living, including cooking, cleaning, and self-help. When Eric and his brother agreed that he had learned as much as he could in the situation, he moved to a small group home, where he became something of a big brother and leader for his housemates. Before long, after developing skills to manage his own money and medications, Eric got his own apartment, where he lived for the rest of his life. His relationship with his brother evolved from one of big brother/little brother to "just two guys" who enjoyed time together in such activities as watching sporting events.

During his lifetime Eric learned to understand his disabilities and went on to become independent and self-reliant. He was, his brother says, "outgrowing" his disabilities, and became interested in helping others. To that end, he became someone who answered questions for others online, and extended himself in generous ways to help. Although he experienced some difficulty in knowing how to interact with others, he learned how to make people welcome, and always gave others the benefit of the doubt in his dealings with them. He loved people, bowling, and cats.

Eric worked at a recycling center, and all his co-workers attended his funeral. His legacy is one of kindness, willingness to help others with disabilities, and a knack for touching the lives of people without making judgments, even when they judged him. He is also remembered as a person who could set lofty goals and work hard to attain them. He took life, his brother says, as it was given to him, and holidays feel empty without him—"Thank God Eric showed up on my doorstep."

Ray Loomis

Ray Loomis spent 15 years of his young adult life in a large state institution—a facility from which he attempted to escape on numerous occasions. Over several years in the community, Ray had some good times and some difficulties, and he realized that people facing the same problems he had faced needed a group to provide support and help (Webb, 2002; Williams & Schoultz, 1982). After working hard to establish a group and to develop leadership skills, Ray was greeted by only three people at the first meeting; but he persisted, and before long attendance increased, and he became an effective leader. Members learned to set goals and carry out tasks, and when they formalized the group's structure, they elected Ray their president. Project Two, a self-advocacy group governed by its members, was a reality.

Soon the group took steps to create a statewide organization, and four years following Ray's initial idea, the group staged its first state convention. Remarkably, the planning, organization, and staging of the convention were accomplished largely by people who did not read or write, and who required assistance with the tasks of everyday life (Williams & Shoultz, 1982). With supports from advisers and with an ability to complement each other's skills, they had accomplished a goal that many thought impossible. Ray received numerous awards, including recognition by a television station with its annual award for extraordinary community volunteer leadership. And along the way, Ray married and became a father.

But all was not well. Ray was ill, and he learned that he had congestive heart failure that would require surgery to repair a heart valve. There were complications with the surgery, and Ray never regained consciousness. His death was devastating, not only for his wife Nancy and their young son, but also for the community of people to whom he had become so important. Ray's funeral was a statewide gathering of people who knew him and his work. After acknowledging the warmth of Ray's laugh and the sparkle in his eye, citizen advocate Ed Skarnulis said this of Ray: "He knew that someone is sitting on a crowded institution ward somewhere waiting to come home. He knew that someone is staring at a TV set in an apartment, feeling lonely and desperately needing a friend to be with and to talk to" (Williams & Schoultz, 1982, p. 32). Ray became that friend for many of the people whom he both led and befriended. And he left a legacy in his oft-quoted advice:

> *If you think you are handicapped,*
> *you might as well stay indoors.*
> *If you think you are a person,*
> *come out and tell the world.*

Pioneers in the New Moral Community

Disability is one aspect of a person's experience, not the totality of one's existence, prompting Dunn (2014) to point out that people with disability are not heroes, but instead simply people. They value friends, family, and community just as other people do, and disability is a part of the everyday reality of their connection to the context in which they live. Nevertheless, adapting to that reality presents real challenges to many people and their families, sometimes requiring heroic effort. For example, Mark, whose story we discussed earlier in this chapter, often arose in the pre-dawn dark in order to be independent in donning his own leg braces before going to school—a task made laborious and time-consuming by his physical challenges, yet important to his sense of self and autonomy. Elsewhere, others have described support staff as heroes for their efforts to ensure community inclusion for people with ID (Office for People with Developmental Disabilities, 2018). And sometimes people with ID are heroes in the traditional sense of the word, as Perske (1980) noted in describing the efforts of young people with ID who lost their lives while trying to save friends who were drowning. Pioneers in the new moral community will be those who make life better, whether for themselves or others, whether in ordinary or extraordinary ways.

The legacy of some people with ID has been that they made life better for others, even when they found themselves in less than desirable circumstances. Mayo Buckner was one of those people. It was snowing in southwest Iowa on October 15, 1898 when Mayo's mother told him they were leaving on a trip. They took a train to Creston, where they spent the night, then continued early the next morning to Glenwood, where his mother would leave the eight-year-old Mayo at the Iowa Home for Feeble-Minded Children (Wallace, 1958). There he would spend the rest of his life—more than six decades. Many years later, officials would find that Buckner had an IQ of 120, although at the time of his admission he was labeled a "medium-grade imbecile." Buckner soon learned to play the violin, and then a number of other musical instruments. He provided music lessons for children of local townspeople, and sometimes played with the town band. He also became a skilled printer. Despite his talents, however, the institution never helped Mayo Buckner return to the community, even though he requested it on several occasions (Wallace, 1958). Nevertheless, he was remembered as a gentle man, well-read and kind, and his name is memorialized at Glenwood by a street named in his honor. In the face of terrible lifelong injustice, Mayo Buckner managed to live and die with grace and dignity, touching the lives of hundreds of people in his community.

Present-day pioneers are finding a variety of ways to support people with ID, and in the process creating new stories in the community. For example, capitalizing on the world-wide popularity of the coffee shop, and realizing that a coffee shop brings together diverse members of the community, Amy Wright, a North Carolina mother of two children with ID, established a coffee shop named for them. The shop, established in recognition of the employment needs of people with ID, employs 40 people with disabilities, and creates connections with the community to which it makes valued contributions. Its success has spawned two additional locations, employing more people (Toner, 2017). Other coffee shops staffed by people with ID have been established in Iowa (Kilen, 2015), Canada (Inclusion BC, 2018), Vermont (Egan, 2014), and Japan (Café caters to mentally disabled, 2014). These shops represent but one approach to providing meaningful employment support while enhancing community participation.

Other employers are increasingly realizing the business, as well as social, value of hiring people with ID (e.g., Institute for Corporate Productivity, 2014), and a growing number of schools are offering such activities as inclusive athletic teams, intended to offer opportunities to all students (Shriver, 2018). Technological supports also have great potential for improving the lives of people with ID (Wehmeyer, Tassé, Davies, & Stock, 2012), whether assistive technology (designed specifically to support people with disability) or mainstream technology (intended for use by anyone, with or without disability; Goldman, 2017).

We have noted just a few of the kinds of supports and community opportunities that are continuing to enhance the lives of people with ID. As society becomes more adept at providing natural supports and more independent participation in the community, people with ID will experience improved quality of life, more meaningful opportunities to contribute to mainstream culture, and the kind of ordinary lives and legacies that Perske (1980) recognized in saying ". . . the many things they have been able to do with me and for me have outweighed many times the things they could not do. And my relationships with such people have been so rich that my world-view has changed for the better" (p. 77). Pioneers in the new moral community continue to find ways to bridge the gap between what is and what can be. In the process, they are helping people to live satisfying lives and create memorable legacies—to live well and to die well.

Conclusion

In a new moral community, we identify people not by their deficits, but by their strengths. We provide the supports, both natural and specialized, to enhance community participation, and we recognize the contributions of people with ID as friends, neighbors, fellow students, co-workers, and citizens. Self-advocate Nancy Ward (2000) lamented the tendency of some to pity, rather than respect, people with ID because, she said, "They will never be what they can be, because you will see their disability rather than their abilities" (p. 33).

In this chapter we have recognized individuals whose abilities, rather than disabilities, created legacies that continue to have meaning not only to their immediate families and friends, but to a much broader community. That community includes people with and without disability, schools and workplaces, shops and organizations, and community services—both specialized and generic. And in that community, people with ID are employees, employers, taxpayers, shoppers, shopkeepers, students, teachers, sons, daughters, brothers, sisters, parents, spectators, and athletes. Death with dignity also means living with dignity, and the new moral community has no more important aim than that.

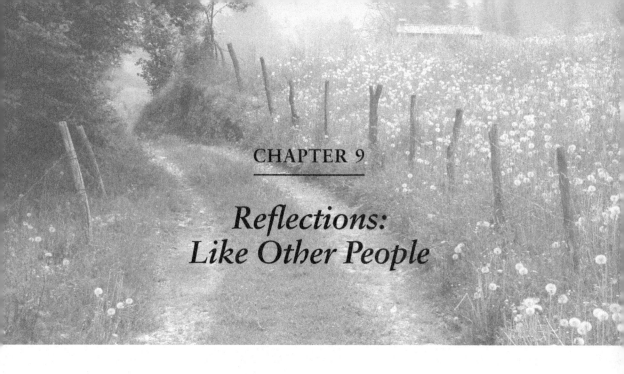

CHAPTER 9

Reflections:
Like Other People

As we reflect upon the lives and legacies of people with ID, we might ask what gives meaning to life, for the person and for family and friends. In Chapter 5 we explored the concept of quality of life—what it means and its role in a new moral community. Other researchers have also examined various aspects of quality of life in relation to the perceived purpose or meaning of life. For example, among middle-aged and older adults, Saha and Ahuja (2017) found a significant relation between life satisfaction and meaning. In a younger group in China, Zhang et al. (2016) identified seven sources of meaning in life: self-development (accomplishing one's aims), social commitment (contributing to society), relationships (with family, friends, and others), secular pursuits (jobs, material possessions, status), life experiences (the joys and sorrows of life), civilization (music, arts, reading, thinking), and autonomy (making decisions, taking charge of own life). It should perhaps not be surprising that these sources of meaning coincide almost completely with personal quality-of-life outcome domains of people with ID (Schalock & Keith, 2016c).

What Matters Most?

Baumeister (1991), discussing meaning in life, set forth four motives that form the foundation of meaning for individuals: purpose (having a goal orientation), value (sense of doing what is moral or right), efficacy (sense of control over life events), and self-worth (feeling of value as a person). These motives, too, are consistent with our understanding of the quality of life of people with ID, and they are a product of the events of daily life (Machell, Kashdan, Short, & Nezlek, 2014). These motives are also evident in the lives of the people whom we have met in this book.

One of Lisa's goals, for example, is to make the country better, to vote for policies that will help to establish equality for all people. Eric, after starting life as an infant with hydrocephalus, became an adult whose goal was to help others with their life challenges. A core value for Ray, when he saw loneliness in people struggling to adjust to community life, was the compassion that drove him to do something to help. And Randy, despite misgivings about the state of world affairs, deeply values other people and believes they have the capacity for good. Mark, when facing a medical decision with life-threatening consequences, asserted his own ability to control his destiny, just as Walker, in clearing the table of unwanted objects, controls his. Ollie's sense of self-worth was evident in her insistence that she be treated like anyone else, and that the only label she wanted was her name. Likewise, Tom's self-esteem was strong enough to give him courage to speak out in public and to call upon authority figures to respect the rights of people with ID. These are people whose motives and aims are clear, and, like those of all people, expressed in unique individual ways.

Chochinov (2002) discussed the importance of knowing that something of our life will transcend our existence—that we will be remembered, that we will have a legacy. Randy wants to be remembered as someone people in need can talk to, and as a person with a good sense of humor. Similarly, Eric loved people and wanted to help those in need. Mark is remembered as a boy who emerged from a childhood with a diagnosis of profound mental retardation to become an adolescent with a big grin who could read and make decisions about his own medical status. Ollie's legacy is not only that of a proud woman with a long history of work on behalf of others with ID, but also a community center that bears her name. Lisa hopes that people will remember her as happy and kind; and Tom was friendly and thoughtful. Like everyone, these are not perfect people; they are simply people. In discussing Walker, Ian Brown (2009, p. 284) said "I see the face of my boy; I see what is human, and lovely and flawed at once."

The people we have discussed here are of course unique in their personalities, individual psychosocial and physical make-up, home or family situations, and personal experience. But in other ways—in their personal aspirations, their connections to those whom they love, and what they expect of life—they are ordinary; they are like other people. Leigh Worrall, a young woman living in Australia, stated it well in summing up her view of the things that give her a good life: "These include my family, my friends, being independent, and being able to make my own decisions and choices. I also enjoy helping and supporting other people" (Keith & Schalock, 2016a, p. 37).

What Does the New Moral Community Offer?

One of the implications of a morality based in the social construction of ID is recognition that there may be many means to similar ends (Renwick, Brown, & Raphael, 2000). Just as Lisa sometimes travels to work via taxi, at other times on a bus, and occasionally in her father's car, so too are many other aims achieved in variable ways. This is the beauty of the concept of individual supports as people move toward greater participation in the communities that surround them. As we noted earlier, and can see in Figure 1, supports

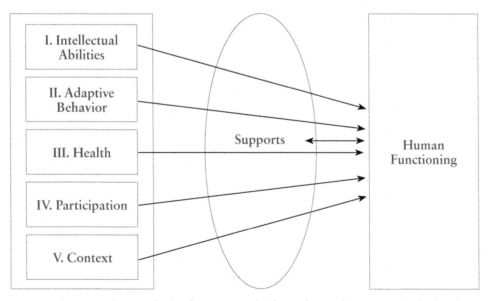

Figure 1. Conceptual view of role of supports in bridging the gap between individual and environmental circumstances and enhanced individual functioning (Schalock et al., 2010)

are the bridge that spans the gap between what is and what can be, between present reality and desired goals. This is a response to the recognition that disability is not simply a matter of impairment, but of the limited opportunity for full participation without support (Stancliffe, Arnold, & Riches, 2016). Different people may achieve participation in many different ways, depending on individual needs and desires, all with the aim of achieving full human potential.

We Are All Human

Kittay (2010), responding to those who argue against the full humanity of people with severe or profound levels of ID, demonstrated an important limitation of the argument, and of the importance of supports. In discussing her daughter, she said:

> I am effectively *showing* what it is impossible to argue. That Sesha is as much a daughter as is any other beloved daughter to a loving parent. That in showing this, I am carrying out my role as her primary caregiver, because I am attempting to win for my daughter the respect and regard that other mothers try to secure for their children (p. 410).

Kittay also argued that no parent of any child, with disability or not, succeeds without support from the community—from schools, social institutions, and other people. Regardless of a child's capacities or needs, she said, parents have an ethical responsibility for the child's welfare, and that responsibility cannot be honored if others do not respect the child as worthy of the same care as other children, and provide the same support. All people want dignity and respect—essential aspects of a new moral community.

Writing in the nineteenth century, Fernald (1893) claimed that people with ID, especially women, were likely to lead "dissolute lives" (p. 212), a claim reflected in the moral arguments of modern-day philosophers who question whether people with severe or profound disability can possess dignity (e.g., Singer, 2010). Yet Kittay (2010), whose daughter was diagnosed with severe to profound ID, wrote movingly of her daughter's love of music and her deep relationships with a range of family, friends, and caregivers. Vorhaus (2017) related examples of people with profound ID and multiple disabilities who can participate meaningfully in exchanges with others, and discussed what we owe to people who can (or potentially can) engage in such interactions. In Chapter 3, we discussed the capabilities approach advocated by Nussbaum (2011). Nussbaum highlighted capabilities she believed would promote quality of life of people with disability, and she too placed emphasis on potential opportunities for growth, understanding the limitations of viewing people in terms of static capacities.

We Are All Capable

The capabilities of people with ID, the abilities that contribute to the legacies that are so important to families and friends, include the capacity to form deep personal relationships (Kittay, 2010), to share accomplishments and sorrows (Wong, 2002), and to live like other people (Groulx, Doré, & Doré, 2000). They may also teach others empathy and patience (Brown, 2009), and achieve academic goals that would not have been possible in the past (Hollingsworth, 2010). Their lives should put to rest the doubts of philosophers who may still debate who is fully human. Sen (1999), in writing about a broad range of vulnerable people, argued that human development depends upon human agency—that all people should be able to exert control over their own lives and to be free of poverty and lack of opportunity. Families and friends of people with ID want these things for them, and they recognize the significance of their lives and legacies.

Successful staff training efforts (e.g., Sandjojo et al., 2008) have assisted people with ID to move toward the kind of personal control that Sen (1999) envisioned. Other efforts (e.g., Embregts, Zijlmans, Gerits, & Bosman, 2017), focused on increasing the emotional intelligence of staff, have shown an ability to increase support that staff provide for emotional relationships, autonomy, and competence.

The Dignity of Risk

The Convention on the Rights of Persons with Disabilities (United Nations, 2006) highlights the importance of providing people with disabilities the same opportunities as others for participation in ordinary social and economic life, and the Convention on the Rights of the Child (United Nations, 1989) states that all children, including those with disabilities, should be free from discrimination. One aspect of full participation is the risk inherent in normal life, and service providers and families supporting individuals with ID should understand the dignity associated with responsible risk. Transportation, workplaces, schools, shopping centers, and a myriad of other settings of everyday life come with some level of risk, and it is incumbent on those supporting people with ID to balance risk against the welfare of the individual and such other factors as the safety of others, other rights of the person (e.g., privacy), and the limits of the care provider (ACIA, 2017). Over-protective approaches to care can deprive people of the dignity of normal life. Perske (1972) summed up the importance of the dignity of risk in this way:

> The world in which we live is not always safe, secure, and predictable. It does not always say "please" or "excuse me." Everyday there is a possibility of being thrown up against a situation where we may have to risk everything, even our lives. This is the *real* world. We must work to develop every human resource within us in order to prepare for these days (p. 5).

Environments have often been built to confine, shelter, and protect people with ID. Although people should be safe, language, architecture, and public attitudes can all convey important messages about expectations for people with ID, as Wolfensberger (1969) noted in discussing the "language of a building." They can send a message of helplessness and hopelessness, or they can suggest, as Ray Loomis admonished his fellow citizens, that people should come out into the world. No one should be subject to irresponsible risk, but the dignity of life is linked to the respect associated with the dignity of reasonable risk.

The Dignity of Dying

Perhaps due to our own fears, we often avoid talking about death, and as a result may dehumanize the dying process (Potthoff, 1972). We owe it to all people, including those with ID, to be honest in discussing and planning for death. Planning for the end of life has become more common among the general population in recent years. However, such planning has been much less common for people with ID. Yet the kind of support that leads to a good death can enable people to feel they have autonomy and to experience the dignity associated with being respected as the end of life approaches (Burke et al., 2017). Discussions about death can be helpful when friends or family die, when death occurs on TV or in movies, and when the death of the person with ID is approaching; the discussions should be in plain, straightforward language that is understandable and meaningful to the person (Burke et al., 2017). Brown (2009) provided a good example of this when he talked with his son Walker about the death of a friend and housemate. It is important to help people to understand and to talk about death, and to realize that they will live on in the memories and lives of the people whom they leave behind (Todd & Read, 2009).

An important aspect of dying and death is the recognition that most people die in ways beyond their control, and there may not be awareness of the moment of death itself, or opportunity for a so-called "good death." Thus, it is left to family and friends to contemplate the meaning of a person's life—that is, to construct the identity of the individual in death (see, e.g., van der Kloot Meijburg, 2005). As we have seen in Chapters 7 and 8, it is not only possible, but desirable, to talk with people with ID and with their families and friends, about how they would like to be remembered—the legacy they hope to leave behind—and about their life satisfactions and memories.

Conclusion

We have suggested the limitations of traditional philosophical views of humanity and morality, and the inadequacies of conceptions of ID that are restricted to biomedical or IQ-based personal characteristics. Instead, the moral community must take account of the capabilities of all people, acknowledge that disability exists as much in the social context as in the individual, and recognize that the community has a responsibility to provide supports that will enable all to participate. The new moral community can enhance the quality of life and the dignity of death for people with ID, and it can recognize their legacies and their importance—to families, friends, communities, and the broader society.

If we think of personhood, with Nussbaum (2006), in terms of unique individual capabilities, we can join those cultures that see capability in good social relations (Azuma & Kashiwagi, 1987; Ruzgis & Grigorenko, 1994); social responsibility (Serpell, Marigan, & Harvey, 1993); meaningful family participation (Super & Harkness, 1982); capacity for caring (Jaworska,

2010); or friendliness (Wober, 1974). To the extent that we can support development of these social goods, we can envision people with ID living full lives, with respect and dignity, in their homes and communities. Growth, relationships, and a rich life in the community are the hallmarks of a new morality, the foundation for living well and dying well, and the basis for a legacy of respect and dignity.

References

Abandoned (2018). *Eastern State Hospital.* Retrieved from: http://abandonedonline.net/
legacy-locations/eastern-state-hospital/

ACIA (2017). Duty of care and dignity of risk. Retrieved from: http://www.acia.net.au/
wp-content/uploads/2016/04/ACIA-017-Balancing-Duty-of-Care-and-Dignity-of-Risk.
pdf

Ahlbom, L. J., Panek, P. E., & Jungers, M. K. (2008). College students' perceptions of persons with intellectual disability at three ages. *Research in Developmental Disabilities, 29,*
61–69. doi: 10.1016/j.ridd.2006.11.001

Ailey, S. H., Brown, P. J., & Ridge, C. M. (2017). Improving hospital care of patients with
intellectual and developmental disabilities. *Disability and Health Journal, 10,* 169–172. doi:
10.1016/j.dhjo.2016.12.019

Aldridge, R. B. (1969). Notes on children's burial grounds in Mayo. *The Journal of the Royal
Society of Antiquaries of Ireland. 99,* 83–87.

Ali, A., Kock, E., Molteno, C., Mfiki, N., King, M., & Strydom, A. (2015). Ethnicity and
self-reported experiences of stigma in adults with intellectual disability in Cape Town,
South Africa. *Journal of Intellectual Disability Research, 59,* 530–540. doi: 10.1111/jir.12158

American Association on Intellectual and Developmental Disabilities (2012a, July
11). Caring at the end of life. Available at: https://aaidd.org/news-policy/policy/
position-statements/caring-at-the-end-of-life#.

American Association on Intellectual and Developmental Disabilities (2012b, July
11). Growth attenuation. Available at: https://aaidd.org/news-policy/policy/
position-statements/growth-attenuation

American Association on Intellectual and Developmental Disabilities (AAIDD; 2015).
Human and civil rights: Joint position statement of AAIDD and The ARC. Retrieved from:
https://aaidd.org/news-policy/policy/position-statements/human-and-civil-rights

Andrews, F. M. (1974). Social indicators of perceived life quality. *Social Indicators Research, 1,*
279–299. doi: 10.1007/BF00303860

Andrews, L. W. (2005, July 1). Hiring people with intellectual disabilities. Society for Human
Resource Management *HR Magazine.* Retrieved from: https://www.shrm.org/hr-today/
news/hr-magazine/pages/0705andrews.aspx

Antlfinger, C. (2015, Sept. 1). Volunteers recognize mentally ill buried in unmarked graves. *The Seattle Times.* Retrieved from: https://www.seattletimes.com/nation-world/volunteers-recognize-mentally-ill-buried-in-unmarked-graves/

Appelbaum, P. S. (2009). Mental retardation and the death penalty: After Atkins. *Psychiatric Services, 60,* 1295–1297. doi: 10.1176/appi.ps60.10,1295

ARC of Nebraska (1998). *1998 Nebraska developmental disabilities service provider profiles.* Lincoln, NE: Author.

ARC of Nebraska (1999). *1999 Nebraska developmental disabilities provider profiles.* Lincoln, NE: Author.

ARC of Nebraska (2000). *2000 Nebraska developmental disabilities provider profiles.* Lincoln, NE Author.

ARC of Nebraska (2001). *2001 Nebraska developmental disabilities provider profiles.* Lincoln, NE: Author.

ARC of Nebraska (2002). *2002 Nebraska developmental disabilities provider profiles.* Lincoln, NE: Author.

ARC of Nebraska (2003). *2003 Nebraska developmental disabilities provider profiles.* Lincoln, NE: Author.

Aristotle (1988). *Politics* (S. Everson, Trans.). Cambridge, UK: Cambridge University Press (original work c. 350 BCE).

Arnold, S. R. C., Riches, V. C., & Stancliffe, R. J. (2011). Intelligence is as intelligence does: Can additional support needs replace disability? *Journal of Intellectual and Developmental Disability, 36,* 254–258. doi: 10.3109/13668250.2011.617732

Arnold, S. R. C., Riches, V. C., Parmenter, T. R., & Stancliffe, R. J. (2009). The I-CAN: Using e-Health to get people the support they need. *Electronic Journal of Health Informatics, 4*(1), e4.

Asmus, J. M., Carter, E. W., Moss, C. K., Biggs, E. E., Bolt, D. M., Born, T. L., . . . Weir, K. (2017). Efficacy and social validity of peer network interventions for high school students with severe disabilities. *American Journal on Intellectual and Developmental Disabilities, 122,* 118–137. doi: 10.1352/1944-7558-122.2.118

Atkins v Virginia 536 U.S. 304 (2002)

Aubert-Marson, D. (2009). Sir Francis Galton: The father of eugenics. *Medecine Sciences, 25,* 641–645. doi: 10.1052/medsci/2009256-7641

Austin, R. D., & Pisano, G. P. (2017). Neurodiversity as a competitive advantage: Why you should embrace it in your workforce. *Harvard Business Review, 95,* 98-103. Retrieved from: https://hbr.org/2017/05/neurodiversity-as-a-competitive-advantage

Axel, K., & Beyer, S. (2013). Supported employment for young people with intellectual disabilities facilitated through peer support: A pilot study. *Journal of Intellectual Disabilities, 17,* 236–251. doi: 10.1177/1744629513495265

Azuma, H., & Kashiwagi, K. (1987). Descriptions for an intelligent person: A Japanese study. *Japanese Psychological Research, 29,* 17–26. doi: 10.4992/psycholres1954.29.17

Barnes, E. (2016). *The minority body: A theory of disability.* Oxford, UK: Oxford University Press.

Barr, M. W. (1899). The how, the why, and the wherefore of the training of feeble-minded children. *Journal of Psycho-Asthenics, 4,* 204–212.

Barr, M. W. (1902a). The imbecile and epileptic *versus* the tax-payer and the community. *Proceedings of the National Conference of Charities and Correction,* 161–165.

Barr, M. W. (1902b). The imperative call of our present to our future. *Journal of Psycho-Asthenics, 7,* 5–8.

Baumeister, R. F. (1991). *Meanings of life.* New York, NY: Guilford Press.

Beadle-Brown, J., Leigh, J., Whelton, B., Richardson, L., Beecham, J., Baumker, T., & Bradshaw, J. (2016). Quality of life and quality of support for people with severe intellectual disability and complex needs. *Journal of Applied Research in Intellectual Disabilities, 29,* 409–421. doi: 10.1111/jar.12200

Beart, S., Hardy, G., & Buchan, L. (2005). How people with intellectual disabilities view their social identity: A review of the literature. *Journal of Applied Research in Intellectual Disabilities, 18,* 47–56. doi: 10.1111/j.1468-3148.2004.00218.x

Beighton, C., & Wills, J. (2017). Are parents identifying positive aspects to parenting their child with an intellectual disability or are they just coping? A qualitative exploration. *Journal of Intellectual Disabilities, 21,* 325–345. doi: 10.1177/1744629516656073

Beirne-Smith, M., Patton, J. R., & Ittenbach, R. (1994). *Mental retardation* (4th ed.). New York, NY: Merrill.

Bejoian, L. M. (2006). Nondualistic paradigms in disability studies & Buddhism: Creating bridges for theoretical practice. *Disability Studies Quarterly, 26,* (3). doi: 10.18061/dsq. v26i3

Bekkema, N., de Veer, A. J. E., Hertogh, C. M. P. M., & Francke, A. L. (2014). Respecting autonomy in the end-of-life care of people with intellectual disabilities: A qualitative multiple-case study. *Journal of Intellectual Disability Research, 58,* 368–380. doi: 0.1111/jir.12023

Berkson, G. (2006). Mental disabilities in western civilization from ancient Rome to the Prerogativa Regis. *Mental Retardation, 44,* 28–40.

Bertoli, M., Biasini, G., Calignano, M. T., Celani, G., De Grossi, G.,Digillo, M. C., . . . Zuccala, G. (2011). Needs and challenges of daily life for people with Down syndrome residing in the city of Rome, Italy. *Journal of Intellectual Disability Research, 55,* 801–820. doi: 10.1111/j.1365-2788.2011.01432.x

Bérubé, M. (2010). Equality, freedom, and/or justice for all. A response to Martha Nussbaum. In E. F. Kittay & L. Carlson (Eds.), *Cognitive disability and its challenge to moral philosophy* (pp. 97–109). Chichester, UK: Wiley-Blackwell.

Bhopti, A., Brown, T., & Lentin, P. (2016). Family quality of life: A key outcome in early childhood intervention services—A scoping review. *Journal of Early Intervention, 38,* 191–211. doi: 10.1177/1053815116673182

Bigby, C., & Beadle-Brown, J. (2016). Culture in better group homes for people with intellectual disability at severe levels. *Intellectual and Developmental Disabilities, 54,* 316–331. doi: 10.1352/1934-9556-54.5.316

Bigby, C., & Knox, M. (2009). "I want to see the queen": Experiences of service use by ageing people with an intellectual disability. *Australian Social Work, 62,* 216–231. doi: 10.1080/03124070902748910

Bigby, C., & Wiesel, I. (2011). Encounter as a dimension of social inclusion for people with intellectual disability: Beyond and between community presence and participation. *Journal of Intellectual & Developmental Disability, 36,* 263–267. doi: 10.3109/13668250.2011.619166

Bigby, C., Bowers, B., & Webber, R. (2011). Planning and decision making about the future care of older group home residents and transition to residential aged care. *Journal of Intellectual Disability Research, 55,* 777–789. doi: 10.1111/j.1365-2788,2010.01297.x

Bigby, C., Knox, M., Beadle-Brown, J., & Clement, T. (2015). 'We just call them people': Positive regard as a dimension of culture in group homes for people with severe intellectual disability. *Journal of Applied Research in Intellectual Disabilities, 28,* 283–295. doi: 10.1111/jar.12128

Bigby, C., Wilson, N. J., Balandin, S., & Stancliffe, R. J. (2011). Disconnected expectations: Staff, family, and supported employee perspectives about retirement. *Journal of Intellectual and Developmental Disability, 36,* 167–174. doi: 10.3109/13668250.2011.598852

Bingham, J. (2013, Mar. 19). Doctors put lower value on lives of the disabled, study finds. *The Telegraph.* Retrieved from: https://www.telegraph.co.uk/news/health/news/9940870/Doctors-put-lower-value-on-lives-of-the-disabled-study-finds.html

Bishop, K. M., Robinson, L. M., & van Lare, S. (2013). Healthy aging for older adults with intellectual and developmental disabilities. *Journal of Psychosocial Nursing and Mental Health Services, 51,* 15–18. doi: 10.3928/02793695-20121218-02

Bittles, A. H., Petterson, B. A., Sullivan, S. G., Hussain, R., Glasson, E. J., & Montgomery, P. D. (2002). The influence of intellectual disability on life expectancy. *The Journals of Gerontology Series A: Biological Sciences and Medical Sciences, 57,* M-470-M472. doi: 10.1111/j.1468-3148.2006.00350.x

Björnsdóttir, K., Stefánsdóttir, G. V., & Stefánsdóttir, A. (2015). 'It's my life': Autonomy and people with intellectual disabilities. *Journal of Intellectual Disabilities, 19,* 5–21. doi: 10.1177/1744629514564691

Blacher, J., Begum, G. F., Marcoulides, G. A., & Baker, B. L. (2013). Longitudinal perspectives of child positive impact on families: Relationship to disability and culture. *American Journal on Intellectual and Developmental Disabilities, 118,* 141–155. doi: 10.1352/1944-7558-118.2.141

Black, E. (2012). *War against the weak: Eugenics and America's campaign to create a master race.* Washington, DC: Dialog Press.

Blatt, B. (1981). How to destroy lives by telling stories. *Journal of Psychiatric Treatment and Evaluation, 3,* 183–191.

Blatt, B. (1999a). The dark side of the mirror. In S. J. Taylor & S. D. Blatt (Eds.), *In search of the promised land: The collected papers of Burton Blatt* (pp. 11–14). Washington, DC: American Association on Mental Retardation.

Blatt, B. (1999b). How to destroy lives by telling stories. In S. J. Taylor & S. D. Blatt (Eds.), *In search of the promised land: The collected papers of Burton Blatt* (pp. 83–98). Washington, DC: American Association on Mental Retardation.

Blatt, B. (1999c). Man through a turned lens. In S. J. Taylor & S. D. Blatt (Eds.), *In search of the promised land: The collected papers of Burton Blatt* (pp. 71–82). Washington, DC: American Association on Mental Retardation.

Blatt, B. (1999d). This crazy business. In S. J. Taylor & S. D. Blatt (Eds.), *In search of the promised land: The collected papers of Burton Blatt* (pp. 125–143). Washington, DC: American Association on Mental Retardation.

Blatt, B., & Kaplan, F. (1966). *Christmas in purgatory: A photographic essay on mental retardation.* Boston, MA: Allyn & Bacon.

Boffey, D. (2018, Mar. 12). Dutch prosecutors to investigate euthanasia cases after sharp rise. *The Guardian.* Retrieved from: https://www.theguardian.com/world/2018/mar/12/dutch-prosecutors-investigate-euthanasia-cases-sharp-rise-docter-assisted-deaths-netherlands

Bogdan, R. (1988). *Freak show: Presenting human oddities for amusement and profit.* Chicago, IL: The University of Chicago Press.

Bonham, G. S., Basehart, S., Schalock, R. L., Marchand, C. B., Kirchner, N., & Rumenap, J. M. (2004). Consumer-based quality of life assessment: The Maryland Ask Me! Project. *Mental Retardation, 42,* 338–355. doi: 10.1352/0047-6765(2004)42%3C338: CQOLAT%3E2.0.CO;2

Bouche, T., & Rivard, L. (2014, Sept. 18). America's hidden history: The eugenics movement. *Genetics Generation.* Retrieved from: www.nature.com/scitable/forums/genetics-generation/america-s-hidden-history-the-eugenics-movement-123919444

Boyd, C. (2007, Nov. 8). Ceremony at the old Hastings State Hospital cemetery. *MINNPOST.* Retrieved from: https://www.minnpost.com/politics-policy/2007/11/grave-grave-group-restores-minnesotans-forgotten-lives/

Breau, L., & Camfield, C. (2011). Pain disrupts sleep in children and youth with intellectual and developmental disabilities. *Research in Developmental Disabilities, 32,* 2829–2840. doi: 10.1016/j.ridd.2011.05.023

Brown, I. (2009). *The boy in the moon: A father's journey to understand his extraordinary son.* New York, NY: St. Martin's Press.

Brown, I. (2011). The absence of normal "frees us." *Bloom.* Retrieved from: http://bloom-parentingkidswithdisabilities.blogspot.com/2011/07/absence-of-normal-frees-us.html

Buck v. Bell, 274 U.S. 200 (1927).

Buntinx, W. (2016). Adaptive behaviour and support needs. In A. Carr, C. Linehan, G. O'Reilly, P. N. Walsh, & J. McEvoy (Eds.), *Intellectual disability and clinical psychology practice* (2nd ed., pp. 107–135). Abingdon, UK: Routledge.

Buntinx, W. H. E., & Schalock, R. L. (2010). Models of disability, quality of life, and individualized supports: Implications for professional practice in intellectual disability. *Journal of Policy and Practice in Intellectual Disabilities, 7,* 283–294. doi: 10.1111/j.1741-1130.2010.00278.x

Burgdorf, M. P., & Burgdorf, R., Jr. (1975). A history of unequal treatment: The qualifications of handicapped persons as a "suspect class" under the equal protection clause. *Santa Clara Lawyer, 15,* 855–910.

Burke, E., O'Dwyer, C., Ryan, K., McCallion, P., & McCarron, M. (2017). *Glancing back, planning forward, a guide for planning end of life care with people with intellectual disability.* Intellectual disability supplement to The Irish Longitudinal Study on Ageing. Dublin, Ireland: Trinity College.

Burton-Smith, R., McVilly, K. R., Yazbeck, M., Parmenter, T. R., & Tsutsui, T. (2009). Quality of life of Australian family carers: Implications for research, policy, and practice. *Journal of Policy and Practice in Intellectual Disabilities, 6,* 189–198. doi: 10.1111/j.1741-1130.2009.00227.x

Butterfield, E. C. (1969). Basic facts about public residential facilities for the mentally retarded. In R. B. Kugel & W. Wolfensberger (Eds.), *Changing patterns in residential services for the mentally retarded.* Washington, DC: President's Committee on Mental Retardation.

Buys, L. R., & Rushworth, J. S. (1997). Community services available to older adults with intellectual disabilities. *Journal of Intellectual and Developmental Disability, 22,* 29–37. doi: 10.1080/13668259700033271

Buys, L., Boulton-Lewis, G., Tedman-Jones, J., Edwards, H., & Knox, M. (2008). Issues of active ageing: Perceptions of older people with lifelong intellectual disability. *Australasian Journal on Ageing, 27,* 67–71. doi: 10.1111/j.1741-6612.2006.00287.x

Café caters to mentally disabled. (2014, June 19). *Japan Times.* Retrieved from: https://www.japantimes.co.jp/news/2014/06/19/national/cafe-caters-to-mentally-disabled/#.q

Campbell, A. (1976). Subjective measures of well-being. *American Psychologist, 31,* 117–124. doi: 10.1037/0003-066X.31.2.117

Carlson, L. (2009). *The faces of intellectual disability: Philosophical reflections.* Bloomington, IN: Indiana University Press.

Carr, A., & O'Reilly, G. (2016). Lifespan development and the family lifecycle. In A. Carr, C. Linehan, G. O'Reilly, P. N. Walsh, & J. McEvoy (Eds.), *The handbook of intellectual disability and clinical psychology practice* (pp. 45–78). London, UK: Routledge.

Carter, E. W., Boehm, T. L., Biggs, E. E., Annandale, N. H., Taylor, C. E., Loock, A. K., & Liu, R. Y. (2015). Known for my strengths: Positive traits of transition-age youth with intellectual disability and/or autism. *Research and Practice for Persons with Severe Disabilities, 40,* 101-119. doi: 10.1177/1540796915592158

Carter, E. W., Brock, M. E., & Trainer, A. A. (2012). Transition assessment and planning for youth with severe intellectual and developmental disabilities. *The Journal of Special Education, 47,* 245–255. doi: 10.1177/0022466912456241

Charron, P. (1707). *Of wisdom: Three books* (2nd ed., trans. G. Stanhope). London.

Chiu, M. Y. L., Yang, X., Wong, F. H. T., Li, J. H., & Li, J. (2013). Caregiving of children with intellectual disabilities in China—An examination of affiliate stigma and the cultural thesis. *Journal of Intellectual Disability Research, 57,* 1117–1129. doi: 10.1111/j.1365-2788.2012.01624.x

Chochinov, H. M. (2002). Dignity-conserving care—A new model for palliative care. *JAMA, 287,* 2253–2260. doi: 10.1001/jama.287.17.2253

Chowdhury, M., & Benson, B. A. (2011). Deinstitutionalization and quality of life of individuals with intellectual disability: A review of the international literature. *Journal of Policy and Practice in Intellectual Disabilities, 8,* 256–265. doi: 10.1111/j.1741-1130.2011.00325.x

Citizens Commission on Human Rights (2018). *Chronology of psychiatry's role in creating the holocaust.* Retrieved from https://www.cchr.org/documentaries/age-of-fear/creating-the-holocaust.html

Cohen, S. R., Holloway, S. D., Dominguez-Pareto, I., & Kuppermann, M. (2014). Receiving or believing in family support? Contributors to the life quality of Latino and non-Latino families of children with disability. *Journal of Intellectual Disability Research, 58,* 333–345. doi: 10.1111/jir.12016

Coles, R. (1989). *The call of stories: Teaching and moral imagination.* Boston, MA: Houghton Mifflin.

Cummins, R. A. (1995). Assessing quality of life. In R. I. Brown (Ed.), *Quality of life for handicapped people* (pp. 102–120). London, UK: Chapman & Hall.

Cummins, R. A. (1997). *Comprehensive quality of life scale—Intellectual disability* (5th ed.). Melbourne, Australia: Deakin University School of Psychology.

Cummins, R. A. (2001). The subjective well-being of people caring for a family member with a severe disability at home. A review. *Journal of Intellectual & Developmental Disability, 26,* 83–100. doi: 10.1080/13668250020032787

Davis, F. G. (1991). *Who is black? One nation's definition.* University Park, PA: Pennsylvania State University Press.

Death Penalty Information Center (2018). *Part I: History of the death penalty.* Retrieved from: https://deathpenaltyinfo.org/part-i-history-death-penalty

DeFrain, J. (1999). Strong families. *Family Matters, 53,* 6–13.

Dempsey, J. (2000, July 12). Worcester State Hospital Hillside Cemetery renovation project. *Worcester Telegram & Gazette.* Retrieved from: http://www.nekg-vt.com/Shrewsbury/Hillside/hillside.htm

Dennis, M. K., & Washington, K. T. (2018). "Just let me go": End-of-life planning among Ojibwe elders. The Gerontologist, 58, 300–307. doi: 10.1093/geront/gnw151

Dennis, R. (2002). Nonverbal narratives: Listening to people with severe intellectual disability. *Research and Practice for Persons with Severe Disabilities, 27,* 239–249. doi: 10.2511/rpsd.27.4.239

Descartes, R. (1952). *Meditations* (L. LaFleur, Trans.), Upper Saddle River, NJ: Prentice Hall (original work published 1641).

Dew, A. Llewellyn, G., & Gorman, J. (2006). "Having the time of my life": An exploratory study of women with intellectual disability growing older. *Health Care for Women International, 27,* 908–929. doi: 10.1080/07399330600880541

Dewar, R., Cahners, N., Mitchell, C., & Forrow, L. (2015). Hinduism and death with dignity: Historic and contemporary case examples. *The Journal of Clinical Ethics, 26,* 40–47.

Dewey, J. (1896). The reflex arc concept in psychology. *Psychological Review, 3,* 357–370. doi: 10.1037/h0070405

Dewey, J. (1922). *Human nature and conduct.* New York, NY: The Modern Library.

Dewey, J. (1934). *Art as experience.* New York, NY: Putnam.

Dewey, J. (1988). *The public and its problems.* In J. Boydston (Ed.), *The later works of John Dewey, vol. 2* (pp. 235–372). Carbondale, IL: Southern Illinois University Press. (Original work published 1927).

DiConsiglio, J. (2015, April 8). The Holocaust killing centers: An historical nightmare for the disabled. *George Washington University Columbian College of Arts & Sciences Spotlight.* Retrieved from: https://columbian.gwu.edu/holocaust-killing-centers-historical-nightmare-disabled

Ditchman, N., Easton, A. B., Batchos, E., Rafajko, S., & Shah, N. (2017). The impact of culture on attitudes toward the sexuality of people with intellectual disabilities. *Sexuality and Disability, 35,* 245–260. doi: 10.1007/s11195-017-9484-x

Division on Mental Retardation and Developmental Disabilities of the Council for Exceptional Children (1992). *MRDD position statement: Capital punishment and individuals with mental retardation.* Reston, VA: Author.

Dobbs, D. (2007, July 8). The gregarious brain. *NY Times Magazine.* Retrieved from: http://www.nytimes.com/2007/07/08/magazine/08sociability-t.html?pagewanted=all

Dockrill, P. (2017, May 9). Up to 7,000 asylum graves are thought to be hidden under the University of Mississippi. *Science Alert.* Retrieved from: https://www.sciencealert.com/up-to-7-000-asylum-graves-are-estimated-to-be-buried-under-the-university-of-mississippi

Dorozenko, K. P., Roberts, L. D., & Bishop, B. J. (2015). Imposed identities and limited opportunities: Advocacy agency staff perspectives on the construction of their clients with disabilities. *Journal of Intellectual Disabilities, 19,* 282–299. doi: 10.1177/1744629515574210

Dowling, S., Manthorpe, J., & Cowley, S. (2007). Working on person-centred planning: From amber to green light? *Journal of Intellectual Disabilities, 11,* 65–82. doi: 0.1177/1744629507073999

Duc, J. K., Herbert, A. R., & Heussler, H. S. (2017). Paediatric palliative care and intellectual disability—A unique context. *Journal of Applied Research in Intellectual Disabilities, 30,* 1111–1124. doi: 10.1111/jar.12389

Dudley, M., & Gale, F. (2002). Psychiatrists as moral community? Psychiatry under the Nazis and its contemporary relevance. *Australian and New Zealand Journal of Psychiatry, 36,* 585–594. doi: 10.1046/j.1440-1614.2002.01072.x

Duggan, C. (2018, Feb. 5). Families call for church intervention over Whalley grave disturbance fears. *Lancashire Telegraph.* Retrieved from: https://www.lancashiretelegraph.co.uk/news/15919702.families-call-for-church-intervention-over-grave-disturbance-fears/

Dunn, D. S. (2014, Sept. 30). People with disabilities aren't heroes—They're people. *Psychology Benefits Society.* Retrieved from: https://psychologybenefits.org/2014/09/30/people-with-disabilities-arent-heroes-theyre-people/

Dybwad, G. (1999). What went wrong? In M. A. Allard, A. M. Howard, L. E. Vorderer, & A. I. Wells (Eds.), *Ahead of his time: Selected speeches of Gunnar Dybwad* (pp. 67–70). Washington, DC: American Association on Mental Retardation.

Dykens, E. M. (2005). Happiness, well-being, and character strengths: Outcomes for families and siblings of persons with mental retardation. *Mental Retardation, 43,* 360–364. doi:

Eberhardt, J. L., & Randall, J. L. (1997). The essential notion of race. *Psychological Science, 8,* 198-203. doi: 10.1111/j.1467-9280.1997.tb00412.x

Egan, H.P. (2018, Mar. 14). Perky Planet Café will employ people with disabilities. *Seven Days.* Retrieved from: https://www.sevendaysvt.com/vermont/perky-planet-cafe-will-employ-people-with-disabilities/Content?oid=13596011

Elks, M. A. (2005).Visual indictment: A contextual analysis of The Kallikak Family photographs. *Mental Retardation, 43,* 268–280. doi: 10.1352/0047-6765(2005)43%5B268: VIACAO%5D2.0.CO;2

Elphinstone, L. (2018). Cultural competence for teachers and students. In K. D. Keith (Ed.), *Culture across the curriculum: A psychology teacher's handbook* (pp. 46–67). Cambridge, UK: Cambridge University Press.

Emerson, E., & Hatton, C. (1996). Deinstitutionalization in the UK and Ireland: Outcomes for service users. *Journal of Intellectual and Developmental Disability, 21,* 17–37. doi: 10.1080/13668259600033021

Evans, E. C. (1945). Galen the physician as physiognomist. *Transactions and Proceedings of the American Philological Association, 76,* 374–382.

Evans, S. E. (2004). *Forgotten crimes: The Holocaust and people with disabilities.* Chicago, IL: Ivan R. Dee.

Fair Punishment Project (2016, Sept.). *Too broken to fix: Part II: An in-depth look at America's outlier death penalty counties.* Harvard Law School Charles Hamilton Houston Institute for Race & Justice and Criminal Justice Institute. Retrieved from: http://fairpunishment. org/wp-content/uploads/2016/12/FPP-TooBroken_II.pdf

Felce, D. (1997). Defining and applying the concept of quality of life. *Journal of Intellectual Disability Research, 41,* 126–135. doi: 10.1111/j.1365-2788.1997.tb00689.x

Felce, D. (2000). Engagement in activity as an indicator of quality of life in British research. In K. D. Keith & R. L. Schalock (Eds.), *Cross-cultural perspectives on quality of life* (pp. 173–190). Washington, DC: American Association on Mental Retardation.

Ferdinand, R., & Marcus, J. (2002). Doing what we had to do in the 1950s: Parents build the foundation. In R. L. Schalock (Ed.), *Out of the darkness and into the light* (pp. 123–134). Washington, DC: American Association on Mental Retardation.

Fernald, W. E. (1893). The history of the treatment of the feeble-minded. *Proceedings of the National Conference of Charities and Correction* (pp. 203–221). Boston, MA: Geo. H. Ellis Co.

Fernald, W. E. (1902). The Massachusetts Farm Colony for the Feeble-Minded. In I. C. Barrows (Ed.), *Proceedings of the National Conference of Charities and Correction, Twenty-Ninth Session* (pp. 487–490). Boston, MA: Geo. H. Ellis Co.

Fernald, W. E. (1915). What is practical in the way of prevention of mental defect? *Proceedings of the National Conference of Charities and Correction,* 289–297.

Fesko, S. L., Hall, A. C., Quinlan, J., & Jockell, C. (2012). Active aging for individuals with intellectual disability: Meaningful community participation through employment, retirement, service, and volunteerism. *American Journal on Intellectual and Developmental Disabilities, 117,* 497–508. doi: 10.1352/1944-7558-117-06.497

Fesmire, S. (2003). *John Dewey and moral imagination.* Bloomington, IN: Indiana University Press.

Feudtner, C., Kang, T. I., Hexem, K. R., Friedrichsdorf, S. J., Osenga, K., Siden, H., . . . Wolfe, J. (2011). Pediatric palliative care patients: A prospective multicenter cohort study. *Pediatrics, 127,* 1094–1101. doi: 10.1542/peds.2010-3225

Field, G. (2016, Mar. 22). Should parents of children with severe disabilities be allowed to stop their growth? *New York Times Magazine.*

Find a Grave (2018). *Eastern State Hospital Cemetery.* Retrieved from: https://www.findagrave. com/cemetery/2195548/eastern-state-hospital-cemetery

Findler, L., & Vardi, A. (2009). Psychological growth among siblings of children with and without intellectual disabilities. *Intellectual and Developmental Disabilities, 47,* 1–12. doi: 10.1352/2009.47:1-1

Finlay, N. (2000). Outside of life: Traditions of infant burial in Ireland from cillin to cist. *World Archaeology, 31,* 407–422. doi: 10.1080/004382400096929

Fisher, M. H. (2016). Heightened social vulnerability among adults with IDD: Findings, perspectives, and needed interventions. In J. R. Lutzker, K. Guastaferro, & M. L. Benka-Coker (Eds.), *Maltreatment of people with intellectual and developmental disabilities* (pp. 139–162). Washington, DC: American Association on Intellectual and Developmental Disabilities.

Fliesler, N. (2016, Mar. 8). Living with an intellectual disability: One couple's story. *Thriving.* Retrieved from https://thriving.childrenshospital.org/living-intellectual-disability-one-couples-story/

Floyd, F. J., Purcell, S. E., Richardson, S. S., & Kupersmidt, J. B. (2009). Sibling relationship quality and social functioning of children and adolescents with intellectual disability. *American Journal on Intellectual and Developmental Disabilities, 114,* 110–127. doi: 10.1352/2009.114.119-127

Foley, K. F. (2015). Foreword. In E. A. Polloway (Ed.), *The death penalty and intellectual disability* (pp. x–xii). Washington, DC: American Association on Intellectual and Developmental Disabilities.

Forrester-Jones, R. (2013). The road barely taken: Funerals, and people with intellectual disabilities. *Journal of Applied Research in Intellectual Disabilities, 26,* 243–256. doi: 10.1111/jar.12022

Forrester-Jones, R., Beecham, J. K., Barnoux, M., Oliver, D., Couch, E.,& Bates, C.(2017). People with intellectual disabilities at the end of their lives: The case for specialist care? *Journal of Applied Research in Intellectual Disabilities, 30,* 1138–1150. doi: 10.1111/jar.12412

French, L. A. (2005). Mental retardation and the death penalty: The clinical and legal legacy. *Federal Probation, 69*(1). Retrieved from: http://www.uscourts.gov/sites/default/files/69_1_4_0.pdf

Friedlander, H. (1995). *The origins of Nazi genocide: From euthanasia to the final solution.* Chapel Hill, NC: The University of North Carolina Press.

Galton, F. (1869). *Hereditary genius: An inquiry into its laws and consequences.* London, UK: Macmillan.

Garattini, C. (2007). Creating memories: Material culture and infantile death in contemporary Ireland. *Mortality, 12,* 193–206. doi: 10.1080/13576270701255172

Georgiadi, M., Kalyva, E., Kourkoutas, E., & Tsakiris, V. (2012). Young children's attitudes toward peers with intellectual disabilities: Effect of the type of school. *Journal of Applied Research in Intellectual Disabilities, 25,* 531–541. doi: 10.1111/j.1468-3148.2012.00699.x

Gilligan, C. (1982*). In a different voice: Psychological theory and women's development.* Cambridge, MA: Harvard University Press.

Giné, C., Gràcia, M., Vilaseca, R., Beltran, F. S., Balcells-Balcells, A., Montalà, M. D., . . . Mestre, J. M. M. (2015). Family quality of life for people with intellectual disabilities in Catalonia. *Journal of Policy and Practice in Intellectual Disabilities, 12,* 244–254. doi: 10.1111/jppi.12134

Gire, J. (2014). How death imitates life: Cultural influences on conceptions of death and dying. *Online Readings in Psychology and Culture, 6*(2). doi: 10.9707/2307/2307-0919.1120

Gire, J. T. (2019). Cultural variations in perceptions of aging. In K. D. Keith (Ed.), *Cross-cultural psychology: Contemporary themes and perspectives* (2nd ed.). Chichester, UK: Wiley-Blackwell.

Glicksman, S., Goldberg, C., Hamel, C., Shore, R., Wein, A., Wood, D., & Zummo, J. (2017). Rights-based and person-centered approaches to supporting people with intellectual disability: A dialectical model. *Intellectual and Developmental Disabilities, 55,* 181–191. doi: 10.1352/1934-9556-55.3.181

Glover, G., Williams, R., Heslop, P., Oyinlola, J., & Grey, J. (2017). Mortality in people with intellectual disabilities in England. *Journal of Intellectual Disability Research, 61,* 62–74. doi: 10.1111/jir.12314

Goddard, H. H. (1912). *The Kallikak family: A study in the heredity of feeble-mindedness.* New York, NY: Macmillan.

Goddard, H. H. (1913a). The Binet tests in relation to immigration. *Journal of Psycho-Asthenics, 18*(2), 105–110.

Goddard, H. H. (1913b). The hereditary factor in feeble-mindedness. *Institutional Quarterly, 4*(2), 9–11.

Goddard, H. H. (1914). *Feeble-mindedness: Its causes and consequences.* New York, NY: Macmillan.

Goddard, H. H. (1917). Mental tests and the immigrant. *The Journal of Delinquency, 2,* 243–277.

Goldman, A. S. (2017, Mar. 23). Leveraging technology in support of people with intellectual and developmental disabilities. *Social Innovations Journal,* Issue 32. Retrieved from:

http://www.socialinnovationsjournal.org/sectors/101-innovation/2358-leveraging-technology-in-support-of-people-with-intellectual-and-developmental-disabilities

Goldman, T. (2000). AHVA: A self-help organization for the improvement of quality of life of people with disabilities. In K. D. Keith & R. L. Schalock (Eds.), *Cross-cultural perspectives on quality of life* (pp. 45–54). Washington, DC: American Association on Mental Retardation.

Goode, D., Hill, D., Reiss, J., & Bronston, W. (2013). *A history and sociology of the Willowbrook State School*. Washington, DC: American Association on Intellectual and Developmental Disabilities.

Goode, D., & Hogg, J. (1994). Towards an understanding of holistic quality of life in people with profound intellectual and multiple disabilities. In D. Goode (Ed.), *Quality of life for persons with disabilities: International perspectives and issues* (pp. 197–207). Cambridge, MA: Brookline.

Goodey, C. F. (2011). *A history of intelligence and "intellectual disability": The shaping of psychology in early modern Europe*. Surrey, UK: Ashgate.

Gorwitz, K. (1974). Census enumeration of the mentally ill and the mentally retarded in the nineteenth century. *Health Services Reports, 89,* 180–187. doi: 10.2307/4595007

Gosse, L., Griffiths, D., Owen, F., & Feldman, M. (2017). Impact of an individualized planning approach on personal outcomes and supports for persons with intellectual disabilities. *Journal of Policy and Practice in Intellectual Disabilities, 14,* 198–204. doi: 10.1111/jppi.12209

Gould, S. J. (1981). *The mismeasure of man*. New York, NY: Norton.

Grandin, T. (2017). Thinking like animals. In S. J. Armstrong & R. G. Botzler (Eds.), *The animal ethics reader* (pp. 251–253). London, UK: Routledge.

Greenspan, S. (2011). Execution of Joe Arridy: Comments of a forensic expert. *Intellectual and Developmental Disabilities, 49,* 197–202. doi: 10.1352/1934-9556-49.3.197

Greenwood, J. D. (2009). *A conceptual history of psychology*. New York, NY: McGraw-Hill.

Greig, J. R. (2015). *Reconsidering intellectual disability: L'Arche, medical ethics, and Christian friendship*. Washington, D.C.: Georgetown University Press.

Griffiths, J., Weyers, H., & Adams, M. (2008). *Euthanasia and law in Europe*. Oxford, UK: Hart.

Groce, N. E. (1985). *Everyone here spoke sign language: Hereditary deafness on Martha's Vineyard*. Cambridge, MA: Harvard University Press.

Grossman, H. J. (Ed.). (1973). *Manual on terminology and classification in mental retardation*. Washington, DC: American Association on Mental Retardation.

Groulx, R., Doré, R., & Doré, L. (2000). My quality of life as I see it. In K. D. Keith & R. L. Schalock (Eds.), *Cross-cultural perspectives on quality of life* (pp. 23–27). Washington, DC: American Association on Mental Retardation.

Grue, L. (2009). Eugenics and euthanasia—Then and now. *Scandinavian Journal of Disability Research, 12,* 33–45. doi: 10.1080/15017410903076776

Gunther, D., & Diekema, D. (2006). Attenuating growth in children with profound developmental disability: A new approach to an old dilemma. *Archives of Pediatrics and Adolescent Medicine, 160,* 1013–1017. doi: 10.1001/archpedi.160.10.1013

Gurung, R. A. R. (2011). Cultural influences on health. In K. D. Keith (Ed.), *Cross-cultural psychology: Contemporary themes and perspectives* (pp. 259–273). Chichester, UK: Wiley-Blackwell.

Hagan, L. D., Drogin, E. Y., & Guilmette, T. J. (2010). Science rather than advocacy when reporting IQ scores. *Professional Psychology: Research and Practice, 41,* 420–423. doi: 10.1037/a0021077

Hall, A. M., & Theron, L. C. (2016). Resilience processes supporting adolescents with intellectual disability: A multiple case study. *Intellectual and Developmental Disabilities, 54,* 45–62. doi: 10.1352/1934-9556-54.1.45

Hall, D. (2014, May 29). Saving Ireland's forgotten burial sites. *Irish Examiner.* Retrieved from: https://www.irishexaminer.com/farming/life/saving-irelands-forgotten-burial-sites-270192.html

Harnacke, C. (2016). The Ashley treatment: Improving quality of life or infringing dignity and rights? *Bioethics, 30,* 141–150. doi: 10.1111/bioe.12180

Harper, R. S. (2002). Are we really "out of the dark"? In R. L. Schalock (Ed.), *Out of the darkness and into the light* (pp. 221–227). Washington, DC: American Association on Mental Retardation.

Hastings, R. P. (2002). Parental stress and behaviour problems of children with developmental disability. *Journal of Intellectual and Developmental Disability, 27,* 149–160. doi: 10.1080/1366825021000008657

Haveman, M., Tillmann, V., Stoppler, R., Kvas, S., & Monninger, D. (2013). Mobility and public transport use abilities of children and young adults with intellectual disabilities: Results from the 3-Year Nordhorn Public Transportation Intervention Study. *Journal of Policy and Practice in Intellectual Disabilities, 10,* 289–299. doi: 10.1111/jppi.12059

Hawkins, B. A. (1997). Promoting quality of life through leisure and recreation. In R. L. Schalock (Ed.), *Quality of life, vol. II: Application to persons with disabilities* (pp. 117–129). Washington, DC: American Association on Mental Retardation.

Heal, L. W., & Chadsey-Rusch, J. (1985). The Lifestyle Satisfaction Scale (LSS): Assessing individuals' satisfaction with residence, community setting, and associated services. *Applied Research in Mental Retardation, 6,* 475–490. doi: 10.1016/0270-3092(85)90022-0

Hedov, G., Annerén, G., & Wikblad, K. (2002). Swedish parents of children with Down's syndrome. *Scandinavian Journal of Caring Sciences, 16,* 424-430. doi: 10.1046/j.1471-6712. 2002.00109.x

Helle, S. (2000). Quality of life: A personal perspective from Finland. In K. D. Keith & R. L. Schalock (Eds.), *Cross-cultural perspectives on quality of life* (pp. 29–31). Washington, DC: American Association on Mental Retardation.

Hensel, E. (2001). Is satisfaction a valid concept in the assessment of quality of life of people with intellectual disabilities? A review of the literature. *Journal of Applied Research in Intellectual Disabilities, 14,* 311–326. doi: 10.1046/j.1468-3148.2001.00081.x

Herps, M. A. Buntinx, W. H. E., & Curfs, L. M. G. (2013). Individual support planning: Perceptions and expectations of people with intellectual disabilities in the Netherlands. *Journal of Intellectual Disability Research, 57,* 1027–1036. doi: 10.1111/j.1365-2788. 2012.01598.x

Herps, M. A., Buntinx, W. H. E., Schalock, R. L., van Breukelen, G. J. P., & Curfs, L. M. G. (2016). Individual support plans of people with intellectual disabilities in residential services: Content analysis of goals and resources in relation to client characteristics. *Journal of Intellectual Disability Research, 60,* 254–262. doi: 10.1111/jir.12245

Heslop, P., Blair, P., Fleming, P., Hoghton, M., Marriott, A., & Russ, L. (2013). *Confidential inquiry into premature deaths of people with learning disabilities.* Bristol, UK: Norah Fry Research Centre, University of Bristol.

Hester, D. M. (2001). What to Do About the Mere Potential for Disabilities. *American Journal of Bioethics, 1*(3), 1–2. doi: 10.1162/152651601750418215

Hester, D. M. (2010). *End of life care and pragmatic decision making: A bioethical perspective.* Cambridge, UK: Cambridge University Press.

Hillman, A., Donelly, L., Whitaker, A., Dew, A., Stancliffe, R. J., Knox, M., . . . Parmenter, T. R. (2012). Experiencing rights within positive, person-centred support networks of people with intellectual disability in Australia. *Journal of Intellectual Disability Research, 56,* 1065–1075. doi: 10.1111/j.1365-2788.2012.01647.x

Hodapp, R. M. (2002). Parenting children with mental retardation. In M. H. Bornstein (Ed.), *Handbook of parenting: Children and parenting* (pp. 355–381). Mahwah, NJ: Lawrence Erlbaum.

Hofstede, G. H. (2001). *Culture's consequences: Comparing values, behaviors, institutions, and organizations across nations* (2nd ed.). Thousand Oaks, CA: Sage.

Holburn, S., Jacobson, J. W., Schwartz, A. A., Flory, M. J., & Vietze, P. M. (2004). The Willowbrook futures project: A longitudinal analysis of person-centered planning. *American Journal on Mental Retardation, 109,* 63-76. doi: 10.1352/0895-8017(2004)109%3C63: TWFPAL%3E2.0.CO;2

Hollingsworth, H. (2010, Oct. 17). Learning independence at college. *San Diego Union-Tribune,* p. A16.

Holocaust Educational Trust (n.d.). *Disabled people and the euthanasia programme.* Retrieved from: http://www.teachers.org.uk/files/disabled-4pp-a4-7927-.pdf

Hu, X., Wang, M., & Fei, X. (2012). Family quality of life of Chinese families of children with intellectual disabilities. *Journal of Intellectual Disability Research, 56,* 30-44. doi: 10.1111/j.1365-2788.2011.01391.x

Hughes, C., & Hwang, B. (1996). Attempts to conceptualize and measure quality of life. In R. L. Schalock (Ed.), *Quality of life: Vol. I. Conceptualization and measurement* (pp. 51–61). Washington, DC: American Association on Mental Retardation.

Hughes, C., Hwang, B., Kim, J., Eisenman, L. T., & Killian, D. J. (1995). Quality of life in applied research: A review and analysis of empirical measures. *American Journal on Mental Retardation, 99,* 623–641.

Hunt, M. (1994). *The story of psychology.* New York, NY: Anchor Books.

Iacono, T., Bigby, C., Unsworth, C., Douglas, J., & Fitzpatrick, P. (2014). A systematic review of hospital experiences of people with intellectual disability. *BMC Health Services Research, 14,* 505. doi: 10.1186/s12912-014-0505-5.

Inclusion BC. (2018). Inclusive coffee shop in Burnaby shines light on employment of people with developmental disabilities. Retrieved from: http://www.inclusionbc.org/employment/whats-new/inclusive-coffee-shop-burnaby-shines-light-employment-people-developmental-disa

Independent (2016, Oct. 24). Argentine woman becomes first nursery teacher with Down's syndrome. Retrieved from: https://thelogicalindian.com/story-feed/get-inspired/argentine-downs-syndrome-woman/

Institute for Corporate Productivity. (2014). *Employing people with intellectual and developmental disabilities.* Seattle, WA: Author.

International Classification of Functioning (2009). *Towards a common language for functioning, disability, and health.* Geneva, Switzerland: World Health Organization.

Itard, J. M. G. (1962/1801). *The wild boy of Aveyron* (trans. G. Humphrey & M. Humphrey). New York, NY: Appleton-Century-Crofts.

James, W. (1995). *Pragmatism.* Mineola, NY: Dover. (Originally published in 1907).

Jarrett, S. (2012). *Disability in time and place.* English Heritage. Retrieved from: https://content.historicengland.org.uk/content/docs/research/disability-in-time-and-place.pdf

Jaworska, A. (2010). Caring and full moral standing redux. In E. F. Kittay & L. Carlson (Eds.), *Cognitive disability and its challenge to moral philosophy* (pp. 369–392). Chichester, UK: Wiley-Blackwell.

Jenkins, R. (1998). Culture, classification and (in)competence. In R. Jenkins (Ed.), *Questions of competence: Culture, classification and intellectual disability* (pp. 1–24). Cambridge, UK: Cambridge University Press.

Ji, L.-J., Zhang, Z., & Nisbett, R. E. (2004). Is it culture or is it language? Examinations of language effects in cross-cultural research on categorization. *Journal of Personality and Social Psychology, 87,* 57–65. doi: 10.1037/0022-3514.87.1.57

Johnson, A. (1899). Concerning a form of degeneracy. II. The education and care of the feeble-minded. *American Journal of Sociology, 4,* 463–473. doi: 10.1086/210821

Johnson, H. (2003, Feb. 16). Unspeakable Conversations. *New York Times.* Retrieved from http://www.nytimes.com/

Jones, J. (2007). Persons with intellectual disabilities in the criminal justice system: Review of issues. *International Journal of Offender Therapy and Comparative Criminology, 51,* 723–733. doi: 10.1177/0306624X07299343

Juhásová, A. (2015). Comparison of quality of life of families with children with disability and families with children without disability. *Procedia-Social and Behavioral Sciences, 174,* 3378–3384. doi: 10.1016/j.sbspro.2015.01.1007

Kant, I. (1983). *Grounding for the metaphysics of morals.* In J. W. Ellington (Ed.), *Immanuel Kant: Ethical philosophy.* Indianapolis, IN: Hackett Publishing Company. (Original work published 1785).

Kath, R. (2016, Nov. 25). Boston woman with Down syndrome starts cookie business, dreams big. Retrieved from: https://boston.cbslocal.com/2016/11/25/boston-woman-down-syndrome-cookie-business-dreams-big/

Keith, H. E., & Keith, K. D. (2013). *Intellectual disability: Ethics, dehumanization, and a new moral community.* Chichester, UK: Wiley-Blackwell.

Keith, J., Bennetto, L., & Rogge, R. D. (2015). The relationships between contact and attitudes: Reducing prejudice toward individuals with intellectual and developmental disabilities. *Research in Developmental Disabilities, 47,* 14–26. doi: 10.1016/j.ridd.2015.07.032

Keith, K. D. (1990). Quality of life: Issues in community integration. In R. L. Schalock (Ed.), *Quality of life: Perspectives and issues* (pp. 93–100). Washington, DC: American Association on Mental Retardation.

Keith, K. D. (2012). Culture and teaching: Lessons from psychology. In J. E. Groccia, M. A. T. Alsudairi, & W. Buskist (Eds.), *Handbook of college and university teaching* (pp. 156–170). Los Angeles, CA: Sage.

Keith, K. D., & Bonham, G. S. (2005). The use of quality of life data at the organization and systems level. *Journal of Intellectual Disability Research, 49,* 799–805. doi: 10.1352/0047-6765(2004)42%3C338:CQOLAT%3E2.0.CO;2

Keith, K. D., Heal, L. W., & Schalock, R. L. (1996). Cross-cultural measurement of critical quality of life concepts. *Journal of Intellectual and Developmental Disabilities, 21,* 273–293. doi: 10.1080/13668259600033201

Keith, K. D., & Schalock, R. L. (2000). Cross-cultural perspectives on quality of life: Trends and themes. In K. D. Keith & R. L. Schalock (Eds.), *Cross-cultural perspectives on quality of life* (pp. 363–380). Washington, DC: American Association on Mental Retardation.

Keith, K. D., & Schalock, R. L. (2016a). People speaking for themselves. In R. L. Schalock & K. D. Keith (Eds.), *Cross-cultural quality of life: Enhancing the lives of people with intellectual disability* (2nd ed.;pp. 35–47). Washington, DC: American Association on Intellectual and Developmental Disabilities.

Keith, K. D., & Schalock, R. L. (2016b). The global perspective on the concept of quality of life. In R. L. Schalock & K. D. Keith (Eds.), *Cross-cultural quality of life: Enhancing the lives of people with intellectual disability* (2nd ed.; pp. 183–189). Washington, DC: American Association on Intellectual and Developmental Disabilities.

Keith, K. D., Schalock, R. L., & Hoffman, K. (1986). *Quality of life: Measurement and programmatic implications.* Lincoln, NE: Region V Mental Retardation Services.

Keyes, D. W., & Edwards, W. J. (1997). Mental retardation and the death penalty: Current status of exemption legislation. *Mental and Physical Disability Law Reporter, 21,* 687–696.

Kilen, M. (2015, Dec. 25). This Des Moines woman is showing that cooking can change lives. *Des Moines Register.* Retrieved from: https://www.desmoinesregister.com/story/life/2015/12/25/des-moines-woman-showing-cooking-can-change-lives/76804470/

King's Fund Centre. (1980). *An ordinary life: Comprehensive locally based services for mentally handicapped people.* London, UK: King Edward's Hospital Fund for London.

Kirkbride, F. B. (1909). Letchworth Village, New York State's new institution for defectives. In A. Johnson (Ed.), *Proceedings of the 36th National Conference of Charities and Corrections* (pp. 85–91). Fort Wayne, IN: Fort Wayne Printing Co.

Kittay, E. F. (2010). The personal is philosophical is political: A philosopher and mother of a cognitively disabled person sends notes from the battlefield. In E. F. Kittay & L. Carlson (Eds.), *Cognitive disability and its challenge to moral philosophy* (pp. 393–413). Chichester, UK: Wiley-Blackwell.

Kittay, E. F. (2011). Forever small: The strange case of Ashley X. *Hypatia, 26*(3), 610–631.

Kon, A. (2008). We cannot accurately predict the extent of an infant's future suffering: the Groningen Protocol is too dangerous to support. *The American Journal of Bioethics, 8,* 27–35. doi: 10.1080/15265160802513150

Kraft, A. (2016, Nov. 1). Teacher with Down syndrome proves that everything is possible. *Parent Herald.* Retrieved from: https://www.parentherald.com/articles/79786/20161101/teacher-with-down-syndrome-proves-that-everything-is-possible.htm

Kuhlmann, F. (1940). One hundred years of special care and training. *American Journal of Mental Deficiency, 45,* 8–24.

Kuhse, H., & Singer, P. (1985). *Should the baby live?* Oxford, UK: Oxford University Press.

Kupfer, J. H. (1983). *Experience as art: Aesthetics in everyday life.* Albany, NY: State University of New York Press.

Lachapelle, Y., Wehmeyer, M. L., Haelewyck, M.-C., Courbois, Y., Keith, K. D., Schalock, R. L., . . . Walsh, P. N. (2005). The relationship between quality of life and self-determination: An international study. *Journal of Intellectual Disability Research, 49,* 740–744. doi: 10.1111/j.1365-2788.2005.00743.x

Lahey, T. (2018, April 5). A harder death for people with intellectual disabilities. *The New York Times.* Retrieved from: https://www.nytimes.com/2018/04/05/well/live/end-of-life-intellectual-disabilities.html

Lakin, K. C. (1979*). Demographic studies of residential facilities for the mentally retarded: An historical review of methodologies and findings.* Minneapolis, MN: University of Minnesota Dept. of Psychoeducational studies.

Lakin, K. C., Jaskulski, T. M., Hill, B. K., Bruininks, R. H., Nemke, M., White, C. C., & Wright, E. A, (1989). *Medicaid services for persons with mental retardation and related conditions.* Minneapolis, MN: Institute on Community Integration, University of Minnesota.

Lakoff, G., & Johnson, M. (1980). *Metaphors we live by.* Chicago, IL: The University of Chicago Press.

Landesman, S. (1986). Quality of life and personal life satisfaction: Definition and measurement issues. *Mental Retardation, 24,* 141–143.

Lawlor, D., Spitz, R., York, M., & Harvey, B. (2013). Using goal analysis to drive improvements in performance and outcomes. *Journal of Intellectual Disabilities, 17,* 301–313. doi: 10.1177/1744629513503590

Lawson, J. (2001). Disability as a cultural identity. *International Studies in Sociology of Education, 11,* 203–222. doi: 10.1080/09620210100200076

Lea, S. J. (1988). Mental retardation: Social construction or clinical reality? *Disability, Handicap, & Society, 3,* 63–69. doi: 10.1080/02674648866780051

Lee, M., Storey, K., Anderson, J. L., Goetz, L., & Zivolich, S. (1997). The effect of mentoring versus job coach instruction on integration in supported employment settings. *Journal of the Association for Persons with Severe Handicaps, 22,* 151–158. doi: 10.1177/154079699702200303

Lekan, T. (2009). Disabilities and educational opportunity: A Deweyan approach. *Transactions of the Charles S. Peirce Society, 45,* 213–230.

Libell, M. (2007). Atkins' wake: How the states have shunned responsibility for the mentally retarded. *Law & Psychology Review, 31,* 155–165.

Lindemann, H. (2010) *Holding one another (well, wrongly, clumsily) in a time of dementia.* In E. F. Kittay & L. Carlson (Eds.), *Cognitive disability and its challenge to moral philosophy* (pp. 163–169). Chichester, UK: Wiley-Blackwell.

Lobar, S. L., Youngblut, J. M., & Brooten, D. (2006). Cross-cultural beliefs, ceremonies, and rituals surrounding death of a loved one. *Pediatric Nursing, 32,* 44–50.

Lodewyks, M. R. (2015, Mar. 11). Strength in diversity: Positive impacts of children with disabilities. *The Vanier Institute of the Family.* Retrieved from: http://vanierinstitute.ca/children-disability-positive-impacts-children-family/

Lonner, W. J. (2013). Cultural competence. In K. D. Keith (Ed.), *The encyclopedia of cross-cultural psychology* (Vol. I, pp. 301–303). Chichester, UK: Wiley-Blackwell.

Lovern, L. (2008). Native American worldview and the discourse on disability. *Essays in Philosophy, 9*(1), article 14.

Luborsky, M. R. (1994). The cultural adversity of physical disability: Erosion of full adult personhood. *Journal of Aging Studies, 8,* 239–253. doi: 10.1016/0890-4065(94)90002-7

Luckasson, R., Borthwick-Duffy, S., Buntinx, W. H. E., Coulter, D. L., Craig, E. M., Reeve, A., . . . Tassé, M. (2002). *Mental retardation: Definition, classification, and systems of support* (10th ed.). Washington, DC: American Association on Mental Retardation.

Lunacy and Idiocy: The Old Law and Its Incubus (1951). *The University of Chicago Law Review, 18,* 361–368. doi: 10.2307/1597690

Lutfiyya, Z. M., & Schwartz, K. D. (2010). Applying the dignity-conserving model. In S. L. Friedman & D/ T. Helm (Eds.), *End-of-life care for children and adults with intellectual and developmental disabilities* (pp. 201–217). Washington, DC: American Association on Intellectual and Developmental Disabilities.

Machell, K. A., Kashdan, T. B., Short, J. L., & Nezlek, J. B. (2014). Relationships between meaning in life, social and achievement events, and positive and negative affect in daily life. *Journal of Personality, 83,* 287–298. doi: 10.1111/jopy.12103

Magee, J. (2012, Oct. 11). Whalley cemetery is a 'national disgrace,' *The Clitheroe Advertiser and Times.* Retrieved from: https://www.clitheroeadvertiser.co.uk/news/whalley-cemetery-is-a-national-disgrace-1-5012993

Manners, P. J., & Carruthers, E. (2006). Living with learning difficulties: Emma's story. *British Journal of Learning Disabilities, 34,* 206–210. doi: 10.1111/j.1468-3156.2006.00392.x

Markus, H. R., & Kitayama, S. (1991). Culture and the self: Implications for cognition, emotion, and motivation. *Psychological Review, 98,* 224–253. doi: 10.1037/0033-295X.98.2.224

Mason, V. A., & Dowling, S. F. (2016). Bereavement in the lives of people with intellectual disabilities. *Intellectual Disability and Health.* Retrieved from: http://www.intellectualdisability.info/life-stages/articles/bereavement-in-the-lives-of-people-with-intellectual-disabilities

Matsumoto, D. (2000). Foreword. In K. D. Keith & R. L. Schalock (Eds.), *Cross-cultural perspectives on quality of life* (pp. xxi–xxiv). Washington, DC: American Association on Mental Retardation.

Matsumoto, D., & Juang, L. (2013). *Culture and psychology* (5th ed.). Belmont, CA: Wadsworth.

McCausland, D., McCallion, P., Cleary, E., & McCarron, M. (2016). Social connections for older people with intellectual disability in Ireland: Results from Wave One of IDS-TILDA. *Journal of Applied Research in Intellectual Disabilities, 29,* 71–82. doi: 10.1111/jar.12159

McConatha, J. T., Schnell, F., Volkwein, K., Riley, L., & Leach, E. (2003).Attitudes toward aging: A comparative analysis of young adults from the United States and Germany. *The International Journal of Aging and Human Development, 57,* 203–215. doi: 10.2190/K8Q8-5549-0Y4K-UGG0

McConkey, R., & Collins, S. (2010). Using personal goal setting to promote the social inclusion of people with intellectual disability living in supported accommodation. *Journal of Intellectual Disability Research, 54,* 135–143. doi: 10.1111/j.1365-2788.2009.01224.x

McDermott, S., & Edwards, R. (2012). Enabling self-determination for older workers with intellectual disabilities in supported employment in Australia. *Journal of Applied Research in Intellectual Disabilities, 25,* 423–432. doi: 10.1111/j.1468-3148.2012.00683.x

McDougall, J., Evans, J., & Baldwin, P. (2010. The importance of self-determination to perceived quality of life for youth and young adults with chronic conditions and disabilities. *Remedial and Special Education, 31,* 252–260. doi: 10.1177/0741932509355989

McElvaney, C. (2011). Client evaluations and summaries: How person-centered planning is tainted by a diagnosis. *Intellectual and Developmental Disabilities, 49,* 203–205. doi: 10.1352/1934-9556-49.3.203

McEvoy, J. (1989). Investigating the concept of death in adults who are mentally handicapped. *British Journal of Mental Subnormality, 35,* 115–121. doi: 10.1179/bjms.1989.016

McEvoy, J., MacHale, R., & Tierney, E. (2012). Concept of death and perceptions of bereavement in adults with intellectual disabilities. *Journal of Intellectual Disability Research, 56,* 191–203. doi: 10.1111/j.1365-2788.2011.01456.x

McEvoy, J., Treacy, B., & Quigley, J. (2017). A matter of life and death: Knowledge about the body and concept of death in adults with intellectual disabilities. *Journal of Intellectual Disability Research, 61,* 89–98. doi: 10.1111/jir.12347

McFarland, J., Hussar, B., Wang, X., Zhang, J., Wang, K., Rathbun, . . . Bullock Mann, F. (2018). *The Condition of Education 2018* (NCES 2018-144). U.S. Department of Education. Washington, DC: National Center for Education Statistics. Retrieved from: https://nces.ed.gov/pubsearch/pubsinfo.asp?pubid=2018144.

McHugh, M. C., & Howard, D. E. (2017). Friendship at any cost: Parent perspectives on cyberbullying children with intellectual and developmental disabilities. *Journal of Mental Health Research in Intellectual Disabilities, 10,* 288–308. doi: 10.1080/19315864.2017.1299268

Mead, G. (1934). *Mind, self and society: From the standpoint of a social behaviorist.* C. Morris (Ed.). Chicago, IL: The University of Chicago Press.

Megret, F. (2008). The disabilities convention: Human rights of persons with disabilities or disability rights? *Human Rights Quarterly, 30,* 494–516. doi: 10.1353/hrq.0.0000

Menolascino, F. J. (1977). *Challenges in mental retardation: Progressive ideology and services.* New York, NY: Human Sciences Press.

Menolascino, F. J., & Egger, M. L. (1978). *Medical dimensions of mental retardation.* Lincoln, NE: University of Nebraska Press.

Miki, K. (2017, May 10). The boy in the moon: Catching up with Ian Brown and Walker seven years later. *Today's Parent.* Retrieved from: https://www.todaysparent.com/family/special-needs/the-boy-in-the-moon-catching-up-with-ian-brown-and-walker-seven-years-later/

Moore, R. M. (2015). Appreciating cultural dimensions and connections in hospice care. *Journal of Social Work in End-of-Life & Palliative Care, 11,* 6–10. doi: 10.1080/15524256.2015.1021069

Morin, D., Rivard, M., Crocker, A. G., Boursier, C. P., & J. Caron (2013). Public attitudes towards intellectual disability: A multidimensional perspective. *Journal of Intellectual Disability Research, 57,* 279–292. doi: 10.1111/jir.12008

Moro, T. T., Savage, T. A., & Gehlert, S. (2017). Agency, social and healthcare supports for adults with intellectual disability at the end of life in out-of-home, non-institutional community residences in Western nations: A literature review. *Journal of Applied Research in Intellectual Disabilities, 30,* 1045–1056. doi: 10.1111/jar.12374

Morisse, E., Vandemaele, E., Claes, C., Claes, L., & Vandevelde, S. (2013). Quality of life in persons with developmental disabilities and mental health problems: An explorative study. *The Scientific World Journal,* Article ID 491918, 8 pages. doi: 10.1155/2013/491918

Mostert, R. (2016). Personal involvement and empowerment. In R. L. Schalock & K. D. Keith (Eds.), *Cross-cultural quality of life: Enhancing the lives of people with intellectual disability* (pp. 49–57). Washington, DC: American Association on Intellectual and Developmental Disabilities.

Mpofu, E. Athanasou, J., Harley, D., Dune, T., Devlieger, P., & Carey, C. D. (2018). Integration of culture in teaching about disability. In K. D. Keith (Ed.), *Culture across the curriculum: A psychology teacher's handbook* (pp. 500–516). Cambridge, UK: Cambridge University Press.

Murdoch, J. M. (1909). Quarantine mental defectives. In A. Johnson (Ed.), *Proceedings of the 36th National Conference of Charities and Corrections* (pp. 64–67). Fort Wayne, IN: Fort Wayne Printing Co.

Murphy, E. M. (2011). Children's burial grounds in Ireland (cillini) and parental emotions toward death. *International Journal of Historical Archaeology, 15,* 409–428. doi: 10.1007/s10761-011-0148-8

Myers, D. G. (1992). *The pursuit of happiness: Who is happy—and why.* New York, NY: William Morrow.

Niemiec, R. M., Shogren, K. A., & Wehmeyer, M. L. (2017). Character strengths and intellectual and developmental disability: A strength-based approach from positive psychology. *Education and Training in Autism and Developmental Disabilities, 51,* 13–25.

Niihori, T., Aoki, Y., Narumi, Y., Neri, G., Cavé, H., Verloes, A., . . . Matsubara, Y. (2006). Germline KRAS and BRAF mutations in cardio-facio-cutaneous syndrome. *Nature Genetics, 38,* 294–296. doi: 10.1038/ng1749

Noack, T., & Fangeroa, H. (2007). Eugenics, euthanasia, and aftermath. *International Journal of Mental Health, 36,* 112–124. doi: 10.2753/IMH0020-7411360111

Noddings, N. (1984). *Caring: A feminine approach to ethics and moral education.* Berkeley, CA: University of California Press.

Nolan, J. (2006). Excavation of a children's burial ground at Torrybaun, Ballina, County Mayo. In J. O'Sullivan & M. Stanley (Eds.), *Settlement, industry and ritual* (pp. 89–101). Dublin, Ireland: National Roads Authority.

Nord, D., Luecking, R., Mank, D., Kiernan, W., & Wray, C. (2013). The state of the science of employment and economic self-sufficiency for people with intellectual and developmental disabilities. *Intellectual and Developmental Disabilities, 51,* 376–384. doi: 10.1352/1934-9556-51.5.376

Norris, R. (2018). Former long-stay residents plead with cemetery developers: 'Let our friends rest in peace.' *Disabled Go News.* Retrieved from: https://www.disabledgo.com/blog/2018/03/former-long-stay-residents-plead-with-cemetery-developers-let-our-friends-rest-in-peace/#.W6z48BsUnIV

Northern Sydney Local Health District (2015). *Death and dying in aboriginal and Torres Strait islander culture.* St. Leonards, Australia: Author.

Nussbaum, M. C. (2006). *Frontiers of justice: Disability, nationality, species membership.* Cambridge, MA: Harvard University Press.

Nussbaum, M. C. (2011). *Creating capabilities: The human development approach.* Cambridge, MA: Harvard University Press.

Nuwer, R. (2014). Mercy for all? *New Scientist, 221*(2958), 28–29. doi: 10.1016/S0262-4079(14)60427-9

O'Brien, C. L., & O'Brien, J. (2002). The origins of person-centered planning. In S. Holburn & P. Vietze (Eds.), *Person-centered planning: Research, practice, and future directions* (pp. 3–27). Baltimore, MD: Brookes.

O'Sullivan, A., & Sheehan, J. (1996). *The Iveragh Peninsula: An archaeological survey of South Kerry.* Cork, Ireland: Cork University Press.

Office for People with Developmental Disabilities. (2018). Everyday heroes. Retrieved from: https://opwdd.ny.gov/opwdd_community_connections/everyday_heroes

Oliver, M. (1996). *Understanding disability: From theory to practice.* Chatham, UK: Mackays.

Page, S. L., & Islam, M. R. (2015). The role of personality variables in predicting attitudes toward people with intellectual disability. *Journal of Intellectual Disability Research, 59,* 741–745. doi: 10.1111/jir.12180

Palmore, E. B. (1982). Attitudes toward the aged: What we know and need to know. *Research on Aging, 4,* 333–348. doi: 10.1177/0164027582004003004

Parent, S., & Shevell, M. (1998). The 'first to perish'. Child euthanasia in the Third Reich. *Archives of Pediatrics and Adolescent Medicine, 152,* 79–86. doi: 10.1001/archpedi.152.1.79

Parkes, C. M., Laungani, P., & Young, B. (1997). Introduction. In C. M. Parkes, P. Laungani, & B. Young (Eds.), *Death and bereavement across cultures* (pp. 3–9). London, UK: Routledge.

Patja, K., Iivanainen, M., Vesala, H., Oksanen, H., & Ruoppila, I. (2000). Life expectancy of people with intellectual disability: A 35-year follow-up study. *Journal of Intellectual Disability Research, 44,* 591–599. doi: 10.1046/j.1365-2788.2000.00280.x

Patti, P., Amble, K., & Flory, M. (2010). Placement, relocation and end of life issues in aging adults with and without Down's syndrome: A retrospective study. *Journal of Intellectual Disability Research, 54,* 538–546. doi: 10.1111/j.1365-2788.2010.01279.x

Patton, K. A., Ware, R., McPherson, L., Emerson, E., & Lennox, N. (2016). Parent related stress of male and female carers of adolescents with intellectual disabilities and carers of children within the general population: A cross-sectional comparison. *Journal of Applied Research in Intellectual Disabilities, 31,* 51–61. doi: 10.1111/jar.12292

Pelleboer-Gunnink, H. A., Van Oorsouw, W. M. W. J., Van Weeghel, J., & Embregts, P. J. C. M. (2017). Mainstream health professionals' stigmatizing attitudes towards people with intellectual disabilities: A systematic review. *Journal of Intellectual Disability Research, 61,* 411–434. doi: 10.1111/jir.12353

Pengra, L. M. (2000). Lakota quality of life: Mitakuye Oyasin. In K. D. Keith & R. L. Schalock (Eds.), *Cross-cultural perspectives on quality of life* (pp. 191–204). Washington, DC: American Association on Mental Retardation.

Perry, D. M. (2018, June 29). How hospitals treat disabled patients. *Pacific Standard.* Retrieved from: https://psmag.com/social-justice/how-hospitals-mistreat-disabled-patients

Perry, J., & Felce, D. (2002). Subjective and objective quality of life assessment: Responsiveness, response bias, and resident: proxy concurrence. *Mental Retardation, 40,* 445–456. doi: 10.1352/0047-6765(2002)040%3C0445:SAOQOL%3E2.0.CO;2

Perry, J., & Felce, D. (2004). Initial finding on the involvement of people with intellectual disability in interviewing their peers about quality of life. *Journal of Intellectual and Developmental Disabilities, 29,* 164–171. doi: 10.1080/13668250410001709502

Perske, R. (1972). The dignity of risk and the mentally retarded. *Mental Retardation 10,* 24–27.

Perske, R. (1980). *New life in the neighborhood: How persons with retardation or other disabilities can help make a good community better.* Nashville, TN: Abingdon.

Perske, R. (2008). False confessions from 53 persons with intellectual disabilities: The list keeps growing. *Intellectual and Developmental Disabilities, 46,* 468–479. doi: 10.1352/2008.46:468-479

Pierce, M., Kilcullen, S., & Duffy, M. (2018). *The situation of younger people with disabilities living in nursing homes in Ireland-phase 1.* Dublin, Ireland: Disability Federation of Ireland & Dublin City University. Available at https://www.disability-federation.ie/

Plichart, M., Barberger-Gateau, P., Tzourio, C., Amouyel, P., Pérès, K., Ritchie, K., . . . Empana, J. P. (2010). Disability and incident coronary heart disease in older community-dwelling adults: The three-city study. *Disability and Incident CHD in Older Adults, 58,* 636–642.

Polloway, E. A., Patton, J. R., & Smith, J. D. (2015). The death penalty and intellectual disability: An introduction. In E. A. Polloway (Ed.), *The death penalty and intellectual disability* (pp. 2–9). Washington, DC: American Association on Intellectual and Developmental Disabilities.

Potthoff, H. H. (1972, April). Ministering to the dying patient. *Ministry: International Journal for Pastors*. Retrieved from: https://www.ministrymagazine.org/archive/1972/04/ministering-to-the-dying-patient

Power, M. J., & Green, A. M. (2010). Development of the WHOQOL disabilities module. *Quality of Life Research, 19,* 571–584. doi: 10.1007/s11136-010-9616-6

President's Council on Bioethics (2008). *Controversies in the determination of death.* Washington, DC: Author.

Prude, A. (2019). Death in Tibetan Buddhism. In T. Knepper, L. Bregman, & M. Gottschalk (Eds.), *Death and dying: Comparative philosophy of religion,* vol. 2 (pp. 125–142). New York, NY: Springer.

Putsch, R. W., III, & Joyce, M. (1990). Dealing with patients from other cultures. In H. K. Walker, W. D. Hall, & J. W. Hurst (Eds.), *Clinical methods: The history, physical, and laboratory examinations* (3rd ed.; pp. 1050–1059). Boston, MA: Butterworths.

Race, D. (2002). The historical context. In D. G. Race (Ed.), *Learning disability: A social approach* (pp. 23–52). London, UK: Routledge.

Rapley, M. (2000). The social construction of "quality of life": The interpersonal production of well-being revisited. In K. D. Keith & R. L. Schalock (Eds.), *Cross-cultural perspectives on quality of life* (pp. 155–172). Washington, DC: American Association on Mental Retardation.

Rapley, M. (2003). *Quality of life research: A critical introduction.* London, UK: Sage.

Rapley, M. (2004). *The social construction of intellectual disability.* Cambridge, UK: Cambridge University Press.

Regan, T. (2004). *The case for animal rights.* Berkeley, CA: University of California Press.

Reid, D. H., Rosswurm, M., & Rotholtz, D. A. (2018). No less worthy: Recommendations for behavior analysts treating adults with intellectual and developmental disabilities with dignity. *Behavior Analysis in Practice, 11.* 71–79. doi: 10.1007/s40617-017-0203-y

Reilly, K. O., & Conliffe, C. (2002). Facilitating future planning for ageing adults with intellectual disabilities using a planning tool that incorporates quality of life domains. *Journal of Gerontological Social Work, 37,* 105–119. doi: 10.1300/J083v37n03_08

Reinders, H. S. (2000). *The future of the disabled in a liberal society: An ethical analysis.* Notre Dame, IN: University of Notre Dame Press.

Reinders, H. S., & Schalock, R. L. (2014). How organizations can enhance the quality of life of their clients and assess their results: The concept of QOL enhancement. *American Journal on Intellectual and Developmental Disabilities, 119,* 291–302. doi: 10.1352/1944-7558-119.4.291

Renwick, R., & Brown, I. (1996). The Centre for Health Promotion's conceptual approach to quality of life: Being, belonging, and becoming. In R. Renwick, I. Brown, & M. Nagler (Eds.), *Quality of life in health promotion and rehabilitation: Conceptual approaches, issues, and applications* (pp. 75–86). Thousand Oaks, CA: Sage.

Renwick, R., Brown, I., & Raphael, D. (2000). Person-centered quality of life: Contributions from Canada to an international understanding. In K. D. Keith & R. L. Schalock (Eds.), *Cross-cultural perspectives on quality of life* (pp. 5–21). Washington, DC: American Association on Mental Retardation.

Reyes, J. M. (2017, Jan. 13). How a loved one was buried in unmarked grave behind a prison, not returned to family. *The News Journal*. Retrieved from: https://www.usatoday.com/story/news/nation-now/2017/01/13/how-loved-one-buried-unmarked-grave-behind-prison-not-returned-family/96552232/

Richards, L. E. (Ed.). (1909). *Letters and journals of Samuel Gridley Howe.* Boston, MA: Dana Estes & Co.

Robertson, J., Emerson, E. Hatton, C., Elliott, J., McIntosh, B., Swift, P., . . . Joyce, T. (2006). Longitudinal analysis of the impact and cost of person-centered planning for people with intellectual disabilities in England. *American Journal on Mental Retardation, 111,* 400–416. doi: 10.1352/0895-8017(2006)111[400:LAOTIA]2.0.CO;2

Robertson, J., Emerson, E., Gregory, N., Hatton, C., Kessissoglou, S., Hallam, A., & Linehan, C. (2001). Social networks of people with mental retardation in residential settings. *Mental Retardation, 39,* 201–214. doi: 10.1352/0047-6765(2001)039<0201:SNO PWM>2,0.CO;2

Rose, D. (2003). Partnership, co-ordination of care and the place of user involvement. *Journal of Mental Health, 12,* 59–70. doi: 10.1080/09638230021000058300

Rushton, P. (1988). Lunatics and idiots: Mental disability, the community, and the poor law in North-East England, 1600–1800. *Medical History, 32,* 34–50. doi: 10.1017/ S0025727300047591

Ruth, R. (2015). Consideration of cultural and linguistic factors. In E. A. Polloway (Ed.), *The death penalty and intellectual disability* (pp. 234–244). Washington, DC: American Association on Intellectual and Developmental Disabilities.

Ruzgis, P., & Grigorenko, E. L. (1994). Cultural meaning systems, intelligence, and personality. In R. J. Sternberg & P. Ruzgis (Eds.), *Personality and intelligence* (pp. 248–270). New York, NY: Cambridge University Press.

Ryan, T. A., & Scior, K. (2016). Medical students' attitudes towards health care for people with intellectual disabilities: A qualitative study. *Journal of Applied Research in Intellectual Disabilities, 29,* 508–518. doi: 10.1111/jar.12206

Ryan, T. G., & Griffiths, S. (2015). Self-advocacy and its impacts for adults with developmental disabilities. *Australian Journal of Adult Learning, 55,* 31–53.

Sack, D. (2015, May 31). The 5 traits of extraordinary ordinary people. *Psychology Today.* Retrieved from: https://www.psychologytoday.com/us/blog/where-science-meets-the-steps/201503/the-5-traits-extraordinary-ordinary-people

Saha, A., & Ahuja, S. (2017). Critical existential thinking, search for meaning and life satisfaction. *Journal of Psychosocial Research, 12,* 187–195. doi: 10.1037/t01069-000

Salekin, K. L., & Everington, C. (2015). Competence to waive Miranda rights and competence to stand trial. In E. A. Polloway (Ed.), *The death penalty and intellectual disability* (pp. 245–262). Washington, DC: American Association on Intellectual and Developmental Disabilities.

Samuel, P. S., Rillotta, F., & Brown, I. (2012. The development of family quality of life concepts and measures. *Journal of Intellectual Disability Research, 56,* 1–16. doi: 10.1111/ j.1365-2788.2011.01486.x

Sanderson, H. (2000). *Person-centred planning: Key features and approaches.* York, UK: Joseph Rowntree Foundation.

Schalock, R. L. (1996). Reconsidering the conceptualization and measurement of quality of life. In R. L. Schalock (Ed.), *Quality of life: Vol. I. Conceptualization and measurement* (pp. 123–139). Washington, DC: American Association on Mental Retardation.

Schalock, R. L., Borthwick-Duffy, S., Bradley, V. J., Buntinx, W. H. E., Coulter, D. L., Craig, E. M., . . . Yeager, M. H. (2010). *Intellectual disability: Definition, classification, and systems of supports* (11th ed.). Washington, DC: American Association on Intellectual and Developmental Disabilities.

Schalock, R. L., Brown, I., Brown, R., Cummins, R. A., Felce, D., Matikka, L., Keith, K. D., & Parmenter, T. (2002). Conceptualization, measurement, and application of quality of life for persons with intellectual disabilities: Report of an international panel of experts. *Mental Retardation, 40,* 457–470. doi: 10.1352/0047-6765(2002)040%3C0457: CMAAOQ%3E2.0.CO;2

Schalock, R. L., & Keith, K. D. (1993). *Quality of life questionnaire.* Worthington, OH: IDS.

Schalock, R. L., & Keith, K. D. (2016a). The evolution of the quality-of-life concept. In R. L. Schalock & K. D. Keith (Eds.), *Cross-cultural quality of life: Enhancing the lives of people with intellectual disability* (2nd ed., pp. 3–12). Washington, DC: American Association on Intellectual and Developmental Disabilities.

Schalock, R. L., & Keith, K. D. (2016b). The role of a quality-of-life theory in a quality-of-life agenda. In R. L. Schalock & K. D. Keith (Eds.), *Cross-cultural quality of life: Enhancing the lives of people with intellectual disability* (2nd ed., pp. 191–201). Washington, DC: American Association on Intellectual and Developmental Disabilities.

Schalock, R. L., & Keith, K. D. (2016c). Setting the cross-cultural quality-of-life agenda to enhance the lives of people with intellectual disability. In R. L. Schalock & K. D. Keith (Eds.), *Cross-cultural quality of life: Enhancing the lives of people with intellectual disability* (2nd ed., pp. 203–217). Washington, DC: American Association on Intellectual and Developmental Disabilities.

Schalock, R. L., Keith, K. D., Verdugo, M. A., & Gomez, L. E. (2010). Quality of life model development and use in the field of intellectual disability. In R. Kober (Ed.), *Quality of life: Theory and implementation* (pp. 17–32). New York, NY: Sage.

Schalock, R. L., Luckasson, R. A., Shogren, K. A., Borthwick-Duffy, S., Bradley, V., Buntinx, W. H. E., . . . Yeager, M. H. (2007). The renaming of mental retardation: Understanding the change to the term *intellectual disability*. *Intellectual and Developmental Disabilities, 45,* 116–124. doi: 10.1352/1934-9556(2007)45[116:TROMRU]2.0.CO.2

Schalock, R. L., & Verdugo, M. A. (2002). *Handbook of quality of life for human service practitioners.* Washington, DC: American Association on Mental Retardation.

Schertz, M., Kami-Visel, Y., Tamir, A., Genizi, J., & Roth, D. (2016). Family quality of life among families with a child who has a severe neurodevelopmental disability: Impact of family and child socio-demographic factors. *Research in Developmental Disabilities, 53/54,* 95–106. doi: 10.1037/t57297-000

Schreiber, S. (2016, Oct. 28). This teacher with Down syndrome is the ultimate inspiration. *Good Housekeeping,* Retrieved from: https://www.goodhousekeeping.com/life/inspirational-stories/news/a41165/noelia-garella-down-syndrome-teacher/

Scior, K. (2011). Public awareness, attitudes and beliefs regarding intellectual disability: A systematic review. *Research in Developmental Disabilities, 32,* 2164–2182. doi: 10.1016/j.ridd.2011.07.005

Scior, K., Addai-Davis, J., Kenyon, M., & Sheridan, J. C. (2013). Stigma, public awareness about intellectual disability and attitudes to inclusion among different ethnic groups. *Journal of Intellectual Disability Research, 57,* 1014–1026. doi: 10.1111/j.1365-2788.2012.01597.x

Scior, K., Kan, K. Y., McLoughlin, A., & Sheridan, J. (2010). Public attitudes toward people with intellectual disabilities: A cross-cultural study. *Intellectual and Developmental Disabilities, 48,* 278–289. doi: 10.1352/1934-9556-48.4.278

Scott, H. M., & Havercamp, S. M. (2014). Mental health for people with intellectual disability: The impact of stress and social support. *American Journal on Intellectual and Developmental Disabilities, 119,* 552–564. doi: 10.1352/1944-7558-119.6.552

Seewooruttun, L., & Scior, K. (2014). Interventions aimed at increasing knowledge and improving attitudes towards people with intellectual disabilities among lay people. *Research in Developmental Disabilities, 35,* 3482–3495. doi: 10.1016/j.ridd.2014.07.028

Séguin, E. (1846). *Traitement moral: Hygiene et éducation des idiots et des autres enfants arriérés.* Paris, France: J. B. Baillière.

Séguin, E. (1907). *Idiocy: And its treatment by the physiological method.* New York, NY: Teachers College, Columbia University (original work 1866).

Sen, A. (1999). *Development as freedom.* New York, NY: Anchor Books.

Seo, H., Shogren, K. A., Wehmeyer, M. L., Little, T. D., & Palmer, S. B. (2017). The impact of medical/behavioral support needs on the supports needed by adolescents with intellectual disability to participate in community life. *American Journal on Intellectual and Developmental Disabilities, 122,* 173–191. doi: 10.1352/1944-7558-122.2.173

Serpell, R., Mariga, L., & Harvey, K. (1993). Mental retardation in African countries: Conceptualization, services and research. *International Review of Research in Mental Retardation, 19,* 1–34. doi: 10.1016/S0074-7750(08)60187-1

Sharma, A. (2002). *The Hindu tradition: Religious beliefs and healthcare decisions.* Park Ridge, IL: The Park Ridge Center for the Study of Health, Faith, and Ethics.

Shaw, K., Cartwright, C., & Craig, J. (2011). The housing and support needs of people with an intellectual disability into older age. *Journal of Intellectual Disability Research, 55,* 895–903. doi: 10.1111/j.1365-2788.2011.01449.x

Sheridan, J., & Scior, K. (2013). Attitudes towards people with intellectual disabilities: A comparison of young people from British South Asian and White British backgrounds. *Research in Developmental Disabilities, 34,* 1240–1247. doi: 10.1016/j.ridd.2012.12.017

Shorter Oxford English Dictionary (2002, 5th ed.). Oxford, UK: Oxford University Press.

Shriver, T. P. (2018, Oct. 21). Let students with disabilities compete in sports with their peers. *The Washington Post.* Retrieved from: https://www.washingtonpost.com/opinions/let-students-with-disabilities-compete-in-sports-with-their-peers/2018/10/21/a4527952-c8e9-11e8-9158-09630a6d8725_story.html?utm_term=.bb89, f9243c6c

Sienkiewicz-Mercer, R. & Kaplan, S. B. (1989). *I raise my eyes to say yes.* Boston, MA: Houghton-Mifflin.

Silvers, A., Waserman, D. T., & Mahowald, M. B. (1998). *Disability, difference, discrimination: Perspectives on justice in bioethics and public policy.* New York, NY: Lanham, Rowman & Littlefield.

Singer, P. (1993). *Practical ethics* (2nd ed.). Cambridge, UK: Cambridge University Press.

Singer, P. (2007, Jan. 26). A convenient truth about disability. *New York Times.* Retrieved from: http://www.nytimes.com/2007/01/26/opinion/26singer.html

Singer, P. (2009). *Animal liberation: The definitive classic of the animal movement.* New York, NY: Harper Perennial Modern Classics. (Original work published 1975).

Singer, P. (2010). Speciesism and moral status. In E. F. Kittay & L. Carlson (Eds.), *Cognitive disability and its challenge to moral philosophy* (pp. 331–344). Chichester, UK: Wiley-Blackwell.

Smith, J. D. (1995). *Pieces of purgatory: Mental retardation in and out of institutions.* Pacific Grove, CA: Brooks/Cole.

Smoker, B. (2003). On advocating infant euthanasia. *Free Inquiry, 24*(1), 17–18.

Soy, A. (2018, Sept. 27). Infanticide in Kenya: "I was told to kill my disabled baby." *BBC News.* Retrieved from: https://www.bbc.com/news/world-africa-45670750

Spiro, J. P. (2009). *Defending the master race.* Lebanon, NH: University Press of New England.

Stancliffe, R. J. (1995). Assessing opportunities for choice-making: A comparison of self- and staff reports. *American Journal on Mental Retardation, 99,* 418–429.

Stancliffe, R. J., Arnold, S. R. C., & Riches, V. C. (2016). The supports paradigm. In R. L. Schalock & K. D. Keith (Eds.), *Cross-cultural quality of life: Enhancing the lives of people with intellectual disability* (pp. 133–142). Washington, DC: American Association on Intellectual and Developmental Disabilities.

Stancliffe, R. J., & Lakin, K. C. (2007). Independent living. In S. L. Odom, R. H. Horner, M. Snell, & J. Blacher (Eds.), *Handbook on developmental disabilities* (pp. 429–448). New York, NY: Guilford Publications, Inc.

Stancliffe, R. J., Lakin, K. C., Larson, S. A., Engler, J., Taub, S., Fortune, J., & Bershadsky, J. (2012). Demographic characteristics, health conditions, and residential service use in adults with Down syndrome in 25 U.S. states. *Intellectual and Developmental Disabilities, 50,* 92–108. doi: 10.1352/1934-9556-50.2.92.

Stangl, R. (2010). Selective Terminations and Respect for the Disabled. *Journal of Medicine & Philosophy, 35,* 32–45. doi: 10.1093/jmp/jhp058

Stein, G. L., & Kerwin, J. (2010). Disability perspectives on health care planning and decision-making. *Journal of Palliative Medicine, 13,* 1059-1064. doi: 10.1089/jpm.2010.0159

Stern, A. M. (2005). Sterilized in the name of public health. *American Journal of Public Health, 95,* 1128–1138. doi: 10.2105/AJPH.2004.041608

Stineman, R., Morningstar, M., Bishop, B., & Turnbull, H. R. (1993). Role of families in transition planning for young adults with disabilities: Toward a method of person-centered planning. *Journal of Vocational Rehabilitation, 3,* 52–61.

Strasser, S. M., Smith, M. O., & O'Quin, K. (2016). Victimization risk of older adults with IDD manifesting later in life: A review of response systems. In J. R. Lutzker, K. Guastaferro, & M. L. Benka-Coker (Eds.), *Maltreatment of people with intellectual and developmental disabilities* (pp. 207–229). Washington, DC: American Association on Intellectual and Developmental Disabilities.

Sullivan, M. (2015, May 11). Westboro hospital ceremony honors those buried with no name. *Worcester Telegram & Gazette.* Retrieved from: http://www.telegram.com/article/20150510/NEWS/150519950

Summers, J. A., Poston, D. J., Turnbull, A. P., Marquis, J., Hoffman, L., Mannan, H., & Wang, M. (2005). Conceptualizing and measuring family quality of life. *Journal of Intellectual Disability Research, 49,* 777–783. doi: 10.1111/j.1365-2788.2005.00751.x

Sundby, S. E. (2014, Dec. 1). The true legacy of Atkins and Roper: The unreliability principle, mentally ill defendants, and the death penalty's unraveling. University of Miami Legal Studies Research Paper No. 15-5. Retrieved from http://papers.ssrn.com/sol3/papers.cfm?abstract_id=2532510

Super, C. M., & Harkness, S. (1982). The infants' niche in rural Kenya and metropolitan America. In L. L. Adler (Ed.), *Cross-cultural research at issue* (pp. 47–55). New York, NY: Academic Press.

Surrey and Borders Partnership. (2012). *A good death 1.* Hove, UK: Pavilion Publishing & Media, Ltd.

Taylor, S. J., & Bogdan, R. (1996). Quality of life and the individual's perspective. In R. L. Schalock (Ed.), *Quality of life: Vol. I. Conceptualization and measurement* (pp. 11–22). Washington, DC: American Association on Mental Retardation.

Terman, L. M. (1916). *The measurement of intelligence: An explanation of and a complete guide for the use of the Stanford revision and extension of* The Binet Simon Intelligence Scale. Boston, MA: Houghton Mifflin.

The Logical Indian (2016, Oct. 27). Shattering stereotypes, Argentine woman becomes first nursery teacher with Down's syndrome. Retrieved from: https://thelogicalindian.com/story-feed/get-inspired/argentine-downs-syndrome-woman/

Thomas, D. H. H. (1957). Cultural attitudes to mental subnormality. *American Journal of Mental Deficiency, 61,* 467–473.

Thompson, D. J., Ryrie, I., & Wright, S. (2004). People with intellectual disabilities living in generic residential services for older people in the U.K. *Journal of Applied Research in Intellectual Disabilities, 17,* 101–108. doi: 10.1111/j.1360-2322.2004.00187.x

Thorndike, E. L. (1939). *Your city.* New York, NY: Harcourt, Brace & Co.

Throne, J. M. (1972). The assessment of intelligence: Towards what end? *Mental Retardation, 10(5),* 9–11.

Tichá, R., Qian, X., Stancliffe, R. J., Larson, S. A., & Bonardi, A. (2018). Alignment between the Convention on the Rights of Persons with Disabilities and the National Core Indicators Adult Consumer Survey. *Journal of Policy and Practice in Intellectual Disabilities, 15,* 247–255. doi: 10.1111/jppi.12260

Todd, S. (2013). 'Being there': The experiences of staff in dealing with matters of dying and death in services for people with intellectual disabilities. *Journal of Applied Research in Intellectual Disabilities, 26,* 215–230. doi: 10.1111/jar.12024

Todd, S., & Read, S. (2009, Sept.). *Death, dying and the intellectual disabilities: Researching the difficult, understanding the painful and sharing the rewards.* Paper presented at the Aging Roundtable, Edinburgh, UK.

Todd, S., Bernal, J., & Forrester-Jones, R. (2013). Death, dying and intellectual disability research. *Journal of Applied Research in Intellectual Disabilities, 26,* 183–185. doi: 10.1111/jar.12027

Toner, K. (2017, Dec. 17). How a cup of coffee becomes a 'human rights movement.' *CNN Heroes.* Retrieved from: https://www.cnn.com/2017/06/22/health/cnnheroes-amy-wright-bitty-and-beaus-coffee/index.html

Totsika, V., Toogood. S., Hastings, R. P., & McCarthy, J. (2010). The effect of active support interactive training on the daily lives of adults with an intellectual disability. *Journal of Applied Research in Intellectual Disabilities, 23,* 112–121. doi: 10.1111/j.1468-3148.2009.00510.x

Trent, J. W., Jr. (1994). *Inventing the feeble mind: A history of mental retardation in the United States.* Berkeley, CA: University of California Press.

Tuffrey-Wijne, I. (2013). *How to break bad news to people with intellectual disabilities: A guide for carers and professionals.* London, UK: Jessica Kingsley Publishers.

Tuffrey-Wijne, I., Hogg, J., & Curfs, L. (2007). End-of-life and palliative care for people with intellectual disabilities who have cancer or other life-limiting illnesses: A review of the literature and available resources. *Journal of Applied Research in Intellectual Disabilities, 20,* 331–344. doi: 10.1111/j.1468-3148.2006.00350.x

Tuffrey-Wijne, I., Giatras, N., Butler, G., Cresswell, A., Manners, P., & Bernal, J. (2013). Developing guidelines for disclosure or non-disclosure of bad news around life-limiting illness and death to people with intellectual disabilities. *Journal of Applied Research in Intellectual Disabilities, 26,* 231–242. doi: 10.1111/jar.12026

Turnbull, A. P., Poston, D. J., Minnes, P., & Summers, A. J. (2007). Providing supports and services that enhance a family's quality of life. In I. Brown & M. Percy (Eds.), *A comprehensive guide to intellectual and developmental disabilities* (pp. 559–569). Baltimore, MD: Paul H. Brookes.

U. S. Department of Justice (2009). *A guide to disability rights laws.* Retrieved from: https://www.ada.gov/cguide.htm

U. S. Equal Employment Opportunity Commission. (2011). Questions & answers about persons with intellectual disabilities in the workplace and the Americans with Disabilities Act. Washington, DC: Author. Retrieved from: https://www.eeoc.gov/laws/types/intellectual_disabilities.cfm

United Nations (1948, Dec. 10). *A Universal Declaration of Human Rights.* New York, NY: Author. Available at: http://undocs.org/A/RES/217(III)

United Nations (1971, Dec. 20). *Declaration on the Rights of Mentally Retarded Persons.* New York, NY: Author. Available at: https://www.ohchr.org/Documents/ProfessionalInterest/res2856.pdf

United Nations (1975, Dec. 9). *Declaration on the Rights of Disabled Persons.* New York, NY: Author. Available at: https://www.ohchr.org/Documents/ProfessionalInterest/res3447.pdf

United Nations (1989, Nov. 20). Convention on the Rights of the Child. New York, NY: Author. Available at: https://www.ohchr.org/en/professionalinterest/pages/crc.aspx

United Nations (2006, Dec. 13). *Convention on the Rights of Persons with Disabilities.* New York, NY: Author. Available at: https://treaties.un.org/doc/source/docs/A_RES_61_106-E.pdf

van der Kloot Meijburg, H. H. (2005). The significance of dying well. *Illness, Crisis and Loss, 13,* 49–62. doi: 10.1177/105413730501300105

Van Hove, G., & Schelfhout, P. (2000). The quality-of-life paradigm in the Flemish-speaking part of Belgium: People with mental retardation finally stand up for themselves. In K. D. Keith & R. L. Schalock (Eds.), *Cross-cultural perspectives on quality of life* (pp. 37–43). Washington, DC: American Association on Mental Retardation.

Van Wagenen, B. (1914). Surgical sterilization as a eugenic measure. *Journal of Psycho-Asthenics, 18,* 185–196.

Vargas, T. (2014, Feb. 11). Ethan Saylor's legacy: Frederick County deputies learn how to interact with disabled. *The Washington Post*. Retrieved from: https://www.washington post.com/local/ethan-saylors-legacy-frederick-co-sheriffs-deputies-learn-how-to-interact-with-disabled/2014/02/11/b0f48eca-92b1-11e3-b46a-5a3d0d2130da_story.html

Vedie, C., & Breathnach, C. S. (2005). The cemetery associated with Leyme Mental Hospital. *History of Psychiatry, 16,* 111–115. doi: 10.1177/0957154X05045256

Verdugo, M. A., Navas, P., Gómez, L. E., & Schalock, R. L. (2012). The concept of quality of life and its role in enhancing human rights in the field of intellectual disability. *Journal of Intellectual Disability Research, 56,* 1036–1045. doi: 10.1111/j.1365-2788.2012.01585.x

Verhagen, E., & Sauer, P. J. J. (2005). The Groningen Project: Euthanasia in severely ill newborn. *The New England Journal of Medicine, 352,* 959–962.

Vorhaus, J. (2017). Sharing in a common life: People with profound and multiple learning difficulties. *Res Publica: A Journal of Legal and Social Philosophy, 23,* 61–79. doi: 10.1080/09687599.2013.831749

Voultsos, P., & Chatzinikolaou, F. (2014). Involuntary euthanasia of severely ill newborns: is the Groningen Protocol really dangerous? *Hippokratia, 18,* 196–203.

Wallace, R. (1958, March 24). Mental homes wrongly hold thousands like Mayo Buckner. *Life, 44*(12), 120–136.

Walsh, P. N. (2000). Quality of life and social inclusion. In K. D. Keith & R. L. Schalock (Eds.), *Cross-cultural perspectives on quality of life* (pp. 315–326). Washington, DC: American Association on Mental Retardation.

Walsh, P. N., Heller, T., Schupf, N., & van Schrojenstein Lantman-de Valk (2001). Healthy ageing—Adults with intellectual disabilities: Women's health and related issues. *Journal of Applied Research in Intellectual Disabilities, 14,* 195–217. doi: 10.1046/j.1468-3148.2001.00070.x

Wang, M., & Brown, R. (2009). Family quality of life: A framework for policy and social service provisions to support families of children with disabilities. *Journal of Family Social Work, 12,* 144–167. doi: 10.1080/10522150902874842

Wang, M., & Kober, R. (2011). Embracing an era of rising family quality of life research. *Journal of Intellectual Disability Research, 55,* 1093–1097. doi: 10.1111/j.1365-2788.2011.01509.x

Ward, N. (2000). The universal power of speaking for oneself. In K. D. Keith & R. L. Schalock (Eds.), *Cross-cultural perspectives on quality of life* (pp. 33–36). Washington, DC: American Association on Mental Retardation.

Wark, S., Hussain, R., & Edwards, H. (2014). The training needs of staff supporting individuals ageing with intellectual disability. *Journal of Applied Research in Intellectual Disabilities, 27,* 273–288. doi: 10.1111/jar.12087

Warren, J. M. (1851, April). An account of two remarkable Indian dwarfs exhibited in Boston under the name of Aztec children. *American Journal of the Medical Sciences*, No. 42, 285–293. doi: 10.1097/00000441-185104000-00001

Watson, S. M. R., & Keith, K. D. (2002). Comparing the quality of life of school-age children with and without disabilities. *Mental Retardation, 40,* 304–312. doi: 10.1352/0047-6765(2002)040%3C0304:CTQOLO%3E2.0.CO;2

Watson, S. M. R., Barreira, A. M., & Watson, T. C. (2000). Perspectives on quality of life: The Brazilian experience. In K. D. Keith & R. L. Schalock (Eds.), *Cross-cultural perspectives on quality of life* (pp. 59–71). Washington, DC: American Association on Mental Retardation.

Webb, O. M. (2002). Call me by my name. In R. L. Schalock (Ed.), *Out of the darkness and into the light* (pp. 55–61). Washington, DC: American Association on Mental Retardation.

Webber, R., Bowers, B., & Bigby, C. (2014). Residential aged care for people with intellectual disability: A matter of perspective. *Australasian Journal on Ageing, 33,* E36–E40. doi: 10.1111/ajag.12086

Wehmeyer, M. L. (2003). Eugenics and sterilization in the heartland. *Mental Retardation, 41,* 57–60. doi: 10.1352/0047-6765(2003)041%3C0057:EASITH%3E2.0.CO;2

Wehmeyer, M. L., & Bolding, N. (2001). Enhanced self-determination of adults with mental retardation as an outcome of moving to community-based work or living environments. *Journal of Intellectual Disability Research, 45,* 1–13. doi: 10.1046/j.1365-2788.2001.00342.x

Wehmeyer, M. L., Buntinx, H. E., Lachapelle, Y., Luckasson, R. A., Schalock, R. L., Verdugo, M. A., . . . Yeager, M. H. (2008). The intellectual disability construct and its relation to human functioning. *Intellectual and Developmental Disabilities, 46,* 311–318. doi: 10.1352/1934-9556(2008)46[311:TIDCAI]2.0.CO.2

Wehmeyer, M., & Schwartz, M. (1998). The relationship between self-determination and quality of life for adults with mental retardation. *Education and Training in Mental Retardation and Developmental Disabilities, 33,* 3–12.

Wehmeyer, M. L., Tassé, M. J., Davies, D. K., & Stock, S. (2012). Support needs of adults with intellectual disability across domains: The role of technology. *Journal of Special Education Technology, 27*(2), 11–22. doi: 10.1177/016264341202700203

Werner, S., & Grayzman, A. (2011). Factors influencing the intention of students to work with individuals with intellectual disabilities. *Research in Developmental Disabilities, 32,* 2502–2510. doi: 10.1016/j.ridd.2011.07.010

Whittaker, J., & Kenworthy, J. (2002). Education services: Why segregated special schools must close. In D. G. Rice (Ed.), *Learning disability—A social approach* (pp. 68–84). London, UK: Routledge.

Widroff, J., & Watson, C. (2008). Mental retardation and the death penalty: Addressing various questions regarding an *Atkins* claim. *Journal of the American Academy of Psychiatry and the Law, 36,* 413–415.

Wiese, M., Dew, A., Stancliffe, R. J., Howarth, G., & Balandin, S. (2013). 'If and when?': The beliefs and experiences of community living staff in supporting older people with intellectual disability to know about dying. *Journal of Intellectual Disability Research, 57,* 980–992. doi: 10.1111/j.1365-2788.2012.01593.x

Wiese, M., Stancliffe, R. J., Balandin, S., Howarth, G., & Dew, A. (2012). End-of-life care and dying: Issues raised by staff supporting older people with intellectual disability in community living services. *Journal of Applied Research in Intellectual Disabilities, 25,* 571–583. doi: 10.1111/jar.12000

Wiese, M., Stancliffe, R. J., Dew, A., Balandin, S., & Howarth, G. (2014). What is talked about? Community living staff experiences of talking with older people with intellectual disability about dying and death. *Journal of Intellectual Disability Research, 58,* 679–690. doi: 10.1111/jir.120665

Wiesel, I., Bigby, C., & Carling-Jenkins, R. (2013). 'Do you think I'm stupid?': Urban encounters between people with and without intellectual disability. *Urban Studies, 50,* 2391–2406. doi: 10.1177/0042098012474521

Wigham, S., Robertson, J., Emerson, E., Hatton, C., Elliott, J., McIntosh, B., . . . Joyce, T. (2008). Reported goal setting and benefits of person centred planning for people with intellectual disabilities. *Journal of Intellectual Disabilities, 12,* 143–152. doi: 10.1177/1744629508090994

Wilfond, B., Miller, P., Korfiatis, C., Diekema, D. Dudzinski, D., Goreing, S., and the Seattle Growth Attenuation and Ethics Working Group (2010, Nov.–Dec.). Navigating growth attenuation in children with profound disabilities: Children's interests, family decision-making, and community concerns. *The Hastings Center Report.* Retrieved from https://www.thehastingscenter.org

Will, G. F. (2012, May 2). Jon Will, 40 years and going with Down syndrome. Washington Post, Retrieved from: https://www.washingtonpost.com/opinions/jon-will-40-years-and-going-with-down-syndrome/2012/05/02/gIQAdGiNxT_story.html?noredirect=on&utm_term=.5f54a2051ca7

Williams, P., & Shoultz, B. (1982). *We can speak for ourselves: Self-advocacy by mentally handicapped people.* London, UK: Souvenir Press.

Wilson, N. J., Stancliffe, R. J., Bigby, C., Balandin, S., & Craig, D. (2010). The potential for active mentoring to support the transition into retirement for older adults with a lifelong disability. *Journal of Intellectual and Developmental Disability, 35,* 211–214. doi: 10.3109/13668250.2010.481784

Wober, M. (1974). Toward an understanding of Kiganda concept of intelligence. In J. W. Berry & P. R. Dasen (Eds.), *Culture and cognition* (pp. 261–280). London, UK: Methuen.

Wolfensberger, W. (1969). The origin and nature of our institutional models. In R. B. Kugel & W. Wolfensberger (Eds.), *Changing patterns in residential services for the mentally retarded* (pp. 59–171b). Washington, DC: President's Committee on Mental Retardation.

Wolfensberger, W. (1975). *The origin and nature of our institutional models.* Syracuse, NY: Human Policy Press.

Wolfensberger, W. (1983). Social role valorization: A proposed new term for the principle of normalization. *Mental Retardation, 21,* 234–239.

Wolfensberger, W. (1988). Common assets of mentally retarded people that are commonly not acknowledged. *Mental Retardation, 26,* 63–70.

Wolfensberger, W. (2000). A brief overview of social role valorization. *Mental Retardation, 38,* 105–123. doi: 10.1352/0047-6765(2000)038<0105:ABOOSR>2.0.CO;2

Wolfensberger, W. (2002a). Needed or at least wanted: Sanity in the language wars. *Mental Retardation, 40,* 75–80. doi: 10.1352/0047-6765(2002)040%3C0075:NOALWS%3E2.0.CO;2

Wolfensberger, W. (2002b). Why Nebraska? In R. L. Schalock (Ed.), *Out of the darkness and into the light* (pp. 23–52). Washington, DC: American Association on Mental Retardation.

Wolfensberger, W. (2011). Social role valorization and, or versus, "empowerment." *Intellectual and Developmental Disabilities, 49,* 469–476. doi: 10.1352/1934-9556-49.6.435

Wolfensberger, W. (2011). Social role valorization: A proposed new term for the principle of normalization. *Intellectual and Developmental Disabilities, 49,* 435–440. doi: 10.1352/1934-9556-49.6.435

Wong, S. (2002). At home with Down syndrome and gender. *Hypatia, 17,* 89–117. doi: 10.1111/j.1527-2001.2002.tb00943.x

World Health Organization (2001). *International classification of functioning, disability, and health (ICF).* Geneva, Switzerland: Author.

World Health Organization (2011). *World report on disability.* Geneva, Switzerland: Author. https://www.theguardian.com/world/2018/mar/12/dutch-prosecutors-investigate-euthanasia-cases-sharp-rise-docter-assisted-deaths-netherlands

Zhang, H., Sang, Z., Chan, D. K. S., Teng, F., Liu, M., Yu, S., & Tian, Y. (2016). Sources of meaning in life among Chinese university students. *Journal of Happiness Studies, 17,* 1473–1492. doi: 10.1007/s10902-015-9653-5

Zoech, I. (2003, October 12). Named: The baby boy who was Nazis' first euthanasia victim. *The Telegraph* (London, UK). Retrieved from: https://www.telegraph.co.uk/education/3319981/Named-the-baby-boy-who-was-Nazis-first-euthanasia-victim.html

Zuckerman, M. (1990). Some dubious premises in research and theory on racial differences. *American Psychologist, 45,* 1297–1303. doi: 10.1037/0003-066X.45.12.1297